THE CATBOAT BOOK

THE CATBOAT BOOK

Edited by

John M. Leavens

Written by

Howard I. Chapelle, John M. Leavens,
Fenwick C. Williams, Edson I. Schock,
Townsend Hornor, Breck Marshall,
Trent H. Holmes, Waldo Howland,
John C. Freeburg, Oscar C. Pease,
John P. Brewer

Published for the Catboat Association
by the International Marine Publishing Company
Camden, Maine

CONTENTS

PREFACE

The catboat is uniquely American. The type evolved as a working boat certainly before 1850 and possibly as far back as the colonial era. It reached its highest perfection of form by 1900.

The evolution of the cat proceeded at an accelerating pace in the last half of the nineteenth century as new uses came into being. For a few brief decades it was popular as a racing boat until the beginning of class racing and the introduction of new and different racing hulls in the 1890's. The gasoline engine brought its use as a working boat to an end in the first decade of the twentieth century. But for its acceptance as a family daysailer and cruising boat, the cat could not have survived to today. The fact is that it did survive and now, under the impetus of mass production, is flourishing as never before.

The catboat, with its huge beam and stubby mast set well forward, was a familiar sight in every harbor from Cape May, New Jersey, to Cape Ann, Massachusetts. Currier and Ives featured the catboat in not one but two popular lithographs of the 1870's. Harbor scene picture postcards of the 1890's and early 1900's show cats nestled alongside whaling ships, awaiting fishing parties at Vineyard and Nantucket wharves or, with sails hoisted to dry, enlivening the waterfront. Joseph C. Lincoln, Cape Cod's popular author, turned out a best seller a year for 40 years and in practically each a catboat appeared.

Perhaps because catboats were seldom registered officially, perhaps because catboat building was a "backyard" industry carried on by individuals in small shops scattered around the northeastern United States seacoast, perhaps because these builders worked from half-hull models with little need or regard for written records, the development of the catboat cannot be traced as readily as can the development of other craft. The fact is that the catboat with its sweet lines and homely qualities was in its day taken for granted as a natural part of the waterfront scene. Even the writers on gaff rig, B. B. Crowninshield, E. P. Morris, and Douglas Phillips-Birt dismiss the catboat with only a few lines. This present book, then, is the first full-dress story of this distinctive American boat—its development, its career as a racer, its design elements and construction details, including the new materials, its restoration, maintenance, and auxiliary power. Knowlegeable people have contributed to this end:

Howard I. Chapelle, Senior Historian Emeritus of the Smithonian Institution and widely known for his books on ships, small craft, boat design, and boatbuilding, writes about the history of the catboat, "where it originated and how it developed."

Fenwick C. Williams was for many years John Alden's designer and has designed more catboats than any other living man. He describes with wit and interest the design elements that make the cat what it is.

Edson I. Schock, now retired from the engineering faculty of the University of Rhode Island, is the second of three successive generations of catboat designers. In classic how-to-do-it manner he tells how to take off the lines of a catboat.

Townsend Hornor, Commodore of the Wianno

Yacht Club in Osterville, Massachusetts, and active in the affairs of the Woods Hole Oceanographic Institution, had the good fortune to be exposed in his boyhood years to the friendly, club-like atmosphere of the Crosby shops. The ties engendered by this happy exposure led to the building of *Frances*, the first Crosby cat to be built in 32 years. She is as pretty a craft as ever sailed Nantucket Sound.

Breck Marshall pioneered the use of fiberglass for catboats. A boyhood spent on Narragansett Bay in sundry catboats, leavened by extensive racing experience both inshore and offshore, and practical exposure in Bill Tripp's yard to fiberglass as a material, uniquely qualified Breck to design three highly successful fiberglass cats and make class racing in catboats a reality for the first time.

Trent H. Holmes, an engineer by profession, turned to ferrocement as a material in the building of *Meow*, the replacement for a big wood cat that had long served him and his family. Boats were built of cement, although with indifferent success, as far back as World War I. Today's ferrocement techniques are a far cry from such early beginnings. Considerable original research went into the design and building of *Meow* and Trent shares his knowledge with all who would join the swing to ferrocement for marine use.

Waldo Howland, a co-founder with his brother Llewellyn of the Concordia Company, builders of the famed Concordia yawls and sloops, carried on the wood-boat traditions of the Beetle Cat for almost 25 of its more than 50 year's existence. His dedication to wood as *the* material for boats is, perhaps, an inheritance from his forebears who were owners of New Bedford whalers and is manifested by his famous schooner *Integrity* and his active membership on the Board of Trustees of the Marine Historical Association, sponsor of Mystic Seaport.

John C. Freeburg, a tool and die maker at Pratt and Whitney Aircraft Company, has had many adventures in *Kiddie Kat*, a 30-foot catboat built in 1927 by Charles Anderson. A decade or so ago he sailed *Kiddie Kat* with his wife, four children, and a dog from Connecticut to Florida and back, returning a year later with a wife, five children, and a dog. In the years since then he has undertaken major rebuilding of *Kiddie Kat,* projects which he describes with knowledge and humor.

John P. Brewer, a professional newspaperman with Associated Press in Boston, is a catboat enthusiast and an assistant editor of the Catboat Association Bulletin. He tells the story of the rebuilding of *Frances*, a 1900 Wilton Crosby catboat in the Mystic Seaport collection, that served as the model for Townie Hornor's new catboat *Frances*, built 68 years later by the Crosby Yacht Building and Storage Company, successor firm to Wilton Crosby.

Oscar C. Pease is the last known catboat fisherman on Martha's Vineyard. He offers bluefishing parties on the Wasque rips to Edgartown summer visitors and in the winter months dredges scallops in Katama Bay. Spring and fall, Oscar works in the boatyard of Norton and Easterbrooks. *Vanity*, his 45-year-old catboat, was built by Manuel Swartz Roberts for Oscar's father. It has been maintained by Oscar with skilled and loving hands since he inherited her. Oscar's practical knowledge of catboats, their rigging, maintenance, and operation is unparalleled and he shares it with modesty and friendly concern. He writes of catboat maintenance and power for catboats.

James Kleinschmidt's watercolor of the catboat *Pinkletink* coasting the Martha's Vineyard shore near Menemsha was painted in the early 1960's when he was assistant curator at Mystic Seaport. Jim is now curator of the Bishop Museum's maritime collection in Honolulu, Oahu, Hawaii. The watercolor is in the possession of *Pinkletink's* owner.

Betty Crosby (Mrs. Wilton B. Crosby, Jr.) of Osterville, Massachusetts, typed the handwritten manuscript, a difficult task in itself and one made more difficult by the fact that the editor's penmanship is the worst that has appeared since Horace Greeley wrote 100 years ago.

Some of the material in this book has been reprinted or adapted, with permission, from articles that first appeared in the bulletins of the Catboat Association. This unusual organization came into being informally in the summer of 1962 and ever since has served as a focal point for the interests of those who share a love for catboats.

John M. Leavens

THE CATBOAT BOOK

Chapter 1

THE CATBOAT
by Howard I. Chapelle

In 1932, I became interested in the history of small boats and, among them, the catboat, which was then in disfavor. There has been a great deal published in the past on catboats but not much about the history of the type, where it originated, and how it developed. I found, as time went on, and as research brought in material, there were many questions that could never be answered accurately.

A great deal has been written about the evolution of the rigs of various types of small boats. There is, for example, the very well-known series of discussions contained in Professor E. P. Morris's history, *The Fore-and-Aft Rig in America* (1927, New Haven, Yale University Press). I discovered, however, that there is a fallacy in the assumption that the development of rigs and hulls in America started at some primitive level and continued through all of the stages possible, as for example, from a spritsail rig to a gaff rig, to a leg-of-mutton rig, to the modern jib-headed rig. This is simply not true historically. All of the rigs, except our extremely high, modern jib-headed rig, were in existence and were in use somewhere in the world at the earliest date of any extensive type-development in North America. This is true of the catboat.

You can show superficial relationships between catboats and, let us say, some of the Dutch boats, some of the English boats, and some of the French boats, but you can't prove that there was an actual relationship among them. The one essential factor in the design of boats proven by history is that they must fit the conditions where they are used and for what they are used. You might have, then, a similar type of boat developing in three or four different places at approximately the same time, without being able to prove, or find any evidence of, copying in one area from the other, or any other relationship. This happens to be true of the catboat.

Catboats are the results of some developments so far in the past that we are not fully informed as to their origin or their progress. The American small boats, in general, started their career of development sometime around 1840. The reason for this is very simple. At this date there began to be sufficient demand for fish to produce local shore fisheries that were profitable for the individual to follow. All boat types that stem from this commercial field, fishing, must have developed as a result of this economic need. No one sits down and tries to figure out how to build a boat that is all-around "better." He tries to figure, instead, how to fit an existing boat so that she will do better the work for which she is required. This was certainly the case with the commercial catboat.

Actually, the record shows that there were at least three different areas in which catboats came into use sometime before 1855. One was in lower New York Bay and in the northern part of New Jersey, including the lagoon area of the Jersey seashore. In these areas there were commercial fisheries requiring shoal-draft craft, and it became the practice to build small centerboarders, half decked, fitted to be operated with two rigs: jib and mainsail sloop, and catboat. We know from actual building records, from half models, and from plans, that these boats

The Point boat built at Newport, Rhode Island, was an early form of catboat. Nathanael Herreshoff sketched her for W. P. Stephens as a deep-keel boat with a full mid-section, slack bilges, raking ends, and a rounded stem profile. Her gaff-rig sail on a slightly raked mast was loose footed on the boom. She also had a running bowsprit on which a jib could be set. (W. P. Stephens, Traditions and Memories of American Yachting.*)*

were in use early in the 1850's, but there is no way of determining when they first came into use.

The reason for building the boats with two rigs was a very practical one. In the summertime, when the winds are relatively light, it is very desirable to have a large sail area and the sloop rig gave this in an easy working form; you could reduce it without having too much of a handful in one large sail, as was the case with the pleasure cat. But in the wintertime (and this is the reverse of what many people expect today) the cat rig was used because it gave a smaller sail spread, which was much easier to handle because the rig was mostly inboard. And, for this reason, the commercial users of cats had quite a different view of their boats than later yachtsmen did. The commercial cat was designed and used for heavy weather work.

Another place where there was very extensive development of the catboat was in Narragansett Bay. Originally, there had been a type of boat called locally the "Newport boat" or "Point boat" — "Newport catboat" was a later expression.

The Newport boat, of which there are at least two known half models, was a very deep keel boat having what we call clipper lines: clipper midsection, straight rising floor, a high bilge, raking ends — and quite sharp ended — with a rounded stem profile. Nathanael Herreshoff remembered these boats and made a sketch for his son L. Francis Herreshoff. He also made a sketch for me at one time. He showed a slightly raking mast, with a loose-footed gaff sail having a boom, and a running bowsprit on which a jib could be set in light weather. This was basically the catboat. Later on, catboats fitted with a centerboard began to be used on Narragansett Bay. There was, however, a large number of keel catboats, and this particular type developed in Narragansett Bay. They were, I think (as far as the evidence goes at least), all built for yachting purposes. This was, of course, the result of a desire to produce a roomy, safe cruising boat for rough water using the catboat rig.

The third area, of course, was Cape Cod and Massachusetts Bay. The late H. Manley Crosby told

Matchless *and another cat tied up across the pier from the whaling bark,* Andrew Hicks. *Matchless of Bourne was built in 1909 at Monument Beach by W. W. Phinney.*

Thelma *swordfishing in 1915. Rodney V. (Rod) Cleveland of Vineyard Haven, Massachusetts, is at the wheel. His father, Charles B. Cleveland, stands on the pulpit, harpoon in hand. The Spanish burton support for the pulpit could be detached to haul a 300-pound swordfish aboard. (Collection of Rodney V. Cleveland)*

Cape May, New Jersey, was the southern extremity of the natural range of the catboat on the Atlantic coast. Will Mills stands on the foredeck of Katharine L *around 1900. Designed for inland waters, this open-cockpit cat features a dishpan bow, a relatively tall, lightly-sparred rig, and an oar to starboard for mud flats. (Collection of Carl Boston)*

Cape May. An open-cockpit daysailer of the 1900's skirts the dunes. (Collection of Carl Boston)

me that his father, Horace S. Crosby (who built the first Crosby catboat with his brother Worthington in the 1850's), saw the first catboat that he had ever seen in Narragansett Bay. He described the boat as being one of the centerboard class there.

In all three areas, the prime purpose of the catboat was fishing. The winter rig, which is the cat rig, was used in the New York sloops. Cats, both keel and centerboard, were used in Narragansett Bay and off Brenton Reef, where it is not always a millpond. Catboats were also used at Martha's Vineyard and in Buzzards Bay, and there again it gets pretty rough. On the Cape, of course, the famous Chatham bar cats built largely by the Crosbys but built by others as well, Bacon for example, faced very rough water and very severe conditions in both wind and weather. The result was that anyone who makes a study of catboat development can pretty well identify, from the half model, the probability of what the model was built for — commercial fishing or yachting. The commercial fishing cats showed markedly straight deadrise and rather soft, high bilges. In profile, of course, they were the typical Cape chopped-off-stern cats, but with very fine easy lines and a relatively small rig. These cats were of light displacement. They gradually changed over the years, under the influence of local racing ideas, and became somewhat flatter in the floor. Also the famous tumblehome stem began to develop in this class of boat. Few of the commercial boats had extremely large rigs, and most of the commercial cats, therefore, steered with a tiller.

It wasn't long, however, before the catboat was accepted as a pleasure boat and, immediately, racing became of interest. This was particularly true in the 1870's and 1880's. Many of the so-called sandbaggers were combination rigs, jib and mainsail for one day's race, cat rig for the next day's

Newly launched 40-foot party cat icebound at H. Manley Crosby's yard, early 1900's. She has the classic lines of the counter-stern, underslung-rudder cat. Her long cockpit and short cabin are characteristic of a party cat. (Collection of the Crosby Yacht Building and Storage Co.)

Lillian, with a large black "L" sewed on her sail, carried passengers and freight from Nantucket Town six miles up harbor to Wauwinet, once with 105 persons aboard. Built in 1888 at Hyannis, she was stretched from 29' 6" to 38' 5". She was still sailing in 1937. (Collection of Charles F. Sayle)

race. This made it possible to enter a number of different races in the same week without having a very difficult transfer job to do. The natural tendency of racing is always to get more sail, more power, and this requires a stiffer, more powerful hull to bear it. As a result, hull development and rig development were taking place at the same time. In the 1880's, particularly, this development of the catboat proceeded very fast and it wasn't long until there were cats afloat with booms so long that a dinghy was needed to pass the clew earring in reefing. It couldn't be reached from the top of the taffrail. Such a boat, obviously, is not suited for cruising or for offshore sailing.

Another thing that entered into the picture at this time was the so-called party boat. In many areas, very large cats were built to carry tourists and summer visitors on short sailing or fishing parties. These were large centerboard cats, some of them up to 42 feet long on deck which resulted in an enormous cat. There were even a few cruising cats built of large size. Charles D. Mower designed one that was 40 feet long on deck.

Racing puts a tremendous emphasis on windward ability, because the actual speed of a boat does not change much except within certain very narrow limitations. The catboat gained favor as a racing boat because of its outstanding ability to go to windward. There is a very simple rule that controls the basic effect of rig on windward ability. As more sails are added that must be trimmed in order to sail to windward, windward ability decreases. Every time a working sail is added, the only way to keep all the sails filled is to let the boat fall off a little. The catboat rig, with its single sail, is thus the most weatherly of all the rigs. Any boat fitted with one sail, whether it's a lateen sail, a lug sail — anything but a square sail, in fact — can be made to stand closer to the wind than a sloop if her sails are equally well cut. Boat for boat and sail for sail, the one-sail boat will point closer to the wind.

If the cat rig is the most weatherly of all rigs, why is it that the catboat has not remained popular as a racing rig? There is a simple reason for this, which also applies to some sloops. In the design of a sail plan for boats of these kinds, there are normally two choices. One choice is to put on a very large working rig so that light sails need not be added to get speed in light weather. The trouble with this choice is that some arrangement has to be made for reefing the rig in heavy weather,

and modern yachtsmen have developed an allergy against reefing. The second choice is to put on more sails in light airs. This solves the problem generally, although it does add to the expense of boating because sails are costly. However, the catboat is unfortunate, since it is very difficult to add anything in the way of a light sail to the cat rig except some type of simple spinnaker. With modern trends in sailing, this is not enough. It would be difficult to make a number of kites that could go on a catboat, largely because they would throw her out of balance, but, in any case, there usually isn't space on the foredeck of a catboat for the handling of light sails. For these reasons, then, the cats are not considered a good racing type today, although they can compete with other rigs under limited conditions where light sails are not permitted.

Windward ability also depends on sail cloth, which is why a modern catboat, other things being equal, will tend to be more weatherly than a catboat of many years ago. A soft sailcloth, easily stretched, won't stand going to windward in a fresh breeze. That's why, in ancient times, the boats did not point as high or sail as fast when brought up close to the wind as they do now. On the other hand, off the wind or reaching, they seem to have been just as fast as a modern boat and, some of them, perhaps a little bit faster. The first improvement in sailcloth was the invention of machine-woven duck, which meant a very hard

On Time, *Frankie Vincent's Crosby cat with 25 girls from the YWCA camp at Makoniky on Martha's Vineyard around 1910. (Collection of John M. Leavens)*

8

Steamboat Wharf, Nantucket, in the early 1880's with a variety of cats in view. The double-ender at the extreme left is an example of a transitional lapstrake, cat-rigged Noman's Land boat. All of the other cats have the long boom typical of Cape Cod cats. Lillian shows up with the "L" on her sail. In the foreground is Capt. Alex Dunham's two-masted, cat-rigged pilot schooner. (Collection of Charles F. Sayle).

cloth. The Americans took advantage of this in the early 1800's to produce more weatherly vessels. This was followed, of course, by improved cutting and, then again, by improved material. Today, we have the synthetic materials, which are very smooth, smoother than duck. Again, we have an opportunity of getting better sails, from the standpoint of performance at least and, I think, in lasting qualities. These things, however, have no particular relation to the hydrodynamics of the hull.

The hull model of a catboat has a limited range of speed. The catboat builder in the old days was his own designer. He designed his hull and rig for the most commonly expected conditions of her use. You can take a catboat and rig her any way and with any quantity of sail you want, but she'll go just so fast and then the additional power is wasted. If you put an engine in a catboat and put in too much power, she just chews up the water. She'll go just as fast and no faster, no matter what power you put in the boat. The only thing we know about sailpower is that the horsepower produced is relatively small. Therefore, the hull that carries that sail must operate at maximum speed for small power, and this determines what a hull should be, which is why the catboat has the shape it has.

People often ask me if changes can be made in a catboat. In general, there is no reason why we should alter the catboat from its basic design. If you want a leg-of-mutton rig on a cat, you can have it, of course. There's nothing to hold you back. It may be more convenient for you, or not, as the case may be, but you can't justify it on the ground that it's a better rig.

There are certain parallels among catboats and such other types as the Noank sloops, the "carry-away" or trap sloops of Eastport, and, to some

Anna W, *Everett A. Poole's catboat, rigged for lobstering under power, at Menemsha in the mid-1930's. (Alan Richardson)*

extent, the overly praised Friendship sloop, the sharpie, the skipjack, and the garvey. Each one of these types was developed for very rigid conditions, under very rigid economic control. If one of these types is used for a yacht, some of the advantages that this boat might have can be obtained if it is used in the area where it was developed. And you can depart from this, in modification. But one of the things that I have learned in trying to combine theoretical study on one hand with practice on the other, is that when I started departing from the original type, I had better have some experience with the original type before I made any decisions. Very often you imagine that this or that won't

work at paper level — drawing board level — to find out a little bit later that it had been working all the while and you didn't recognize the true problem or the solution. I would like to warn all who want to build a catboat, but want to make her different, not to depart too far from the basic catboat design if they want her to be a catboat and have the advantages of a catboat. Every boat, no matter how scientific, no matter how well practiced the designer, is to some extent an experiment, a gamble. If the man who designs the boat is extremely well grounded, the gamble is perhaps less. But it is very difficult to tell sometimes who is well grounded and who is not.

10

Chapter 2

RACING IN CATBOATS
by John M. Leavens

Two eminent authorities, L. Francis Herreshoff and William P. Stephens, contend that catboat racing began in colonial times. No written records of this have yet come to light. However, because men have ever been eager for a test of strength and speed, it is fair to assume that catboat racing began as far back as there were catboats.

L. Francis Herreshoff tells in *Captain Nat Herreshoff* (Sheridan House, New York, 1953) of the 23-foot Point boat *Julia* built by his grandfather, Charles Frederick Herreshoff, at Bristol, Rhode Island in 1833.

"Racing small sailboats," he writes, "had been popular in Narragansett Bay since colonial times, and the general type of craft used was developed at Newport. It was a single-masted craft with the rudder hung on the stern and was heavily ballasted with cobble stones. These boats were called Point boats. . . . This type of boat was later called a catboat when it became popular around New York. . . ."

William P. Stephens corroborates Herreshoff. Writing in *Traditions and Memories of American Yachting* (Motor Boating, Hearst Magazines, Inc., New York, 1942, Second Edition), Stephens quotes a letter written in 1887 to Forest and Stream Publishing Co., for which Stephens had once worked as yachting editor, by Martin Toulman describing the Point boats he had seen in Newport, Rhode Island, as a boy in 1836-8. Stephens adds: " . . . Narragansett Bay is studded with small islands, each with one or more farms, and a sailboat was as essential as a carriage and team to a farmer in a dry country. . . . That, in time, racing should have developed follows as a matter of course, and in *The Spirit of The Times* (a weekly chronicle of the turf, field sports, agriculture, and the stage of 1853), we find an account of a race sailed off Bristol on October 3 of that year. There were 16 starters in four classes, and among the five starters in the third class was the catboat *Julia*."

This recorded race, it will be noted, took place a year after Captain Bob Fish's famous 16-foot, 6-inch racing catboat *Una* was built in Bayonne, New Jersey, and shipped to Cowes, England, where she became so well known through her success as a racer that "Una boat" or unaboat became the English name for the catboat.

The popular small racing boat around New York from 1850 to 1885 was the sandbagger. These were over-canvassed sloops of extremely shoal draft. While Stephens records that sandbaggers under 20 feet raced as catboats, the hull form and the method of sailing were quite alien to the catboat and to the catboat racing that developed elsewhere.

Termination of the Civil War gave yachting a tremendous boost. What had formerly been casual and informal now emerged in new and more lasting form as yacht clubs were organized and regattas and race schedules became the order of the day. In 1871-72, catboat races — as distinct from sandbagger races — under yacht club sponsorship took place at opposite ends of the original range of the catboat: Toms River, New Jersey, and Beverly, Massachusetts. It is likely that similar events were taking place at other points in between. Some

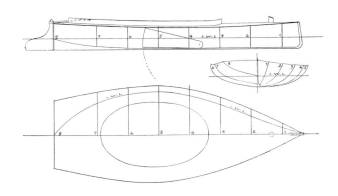

The 16-foot racing catboat Una, *built by Bob Fish of Bayonne, New Jersey in 1852. She was taken by the Marquis of Conyngham to Cowes, England, where she was so successful as a racer that her name became the generic name — unaboat — for catboats in England. (W. P. Stephens,* Traditions and Memories of American Yachting.*)*

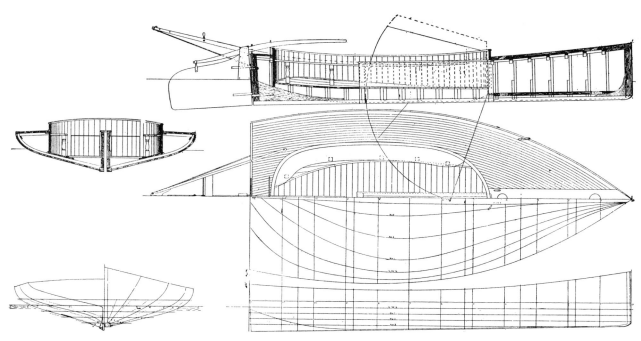

Early sandbaggers were fitted with two mast holes and able to sail as cats or sloops, as circumstances required. This one was built by Neet Willis in 1868. (W. P. Stephens, Traditions and Memories of American Yachting*)*

glass-plate photographs have recently turned up showing eight or ten large cabin catboats racing off the steamboat pier at Cottage City (now Oak Bluffs), Massachusetts, on July 4, 1875. *Camilla,* T. R. Webber's famous 27'5" racing catboat, was launched at New Rochelle, New York, in 1876. Also in 1876, Gil Smith established his yard at Patchogue, Long Island, where he turned out the distinctive catboats that provided keen competition on Great South, Moriches, and Shinnecock

Bays. But it was club organization with weekly races around the circuit that gave catboat racing its first great early boost.

If one individual were to be singled out in connection with the post-Civil War surge of interest in catboat racing, it would have to be Edward Burgess, who later became the designer of three America's Cup defenders: *Puritan* (1885), *Mayflower* (1886), and *Volunteer* (1887). Burgess, born in 1848, was one of seven sons of a well-to-do Bos-

Catboats racing at Cottage City (now Oak Bluffs), Martha's Vineyard in 1875. (Collection of Marshall Cook)

ton sugar merchant. From early youth, the Burgess boys sailed small boats at Sandwich, their summer home on Cape Cod. Among their contemporaries were two Adams boys, George and Charles Francis, grandsons of President John Quincy Adams, and two Bryants, Henry and Dr. John. All four were to become leaders in yachting in the 1880's and 1890's.

Edward Burgess and Nat Herreshoff were the same age. They undoubtedly first met in the mid-1860's when both were students in Cambridge, Massachusetts: Burgess at Harvard and Herreshoff at M.I.T. At the close of the war in 1865, the Boston Yacht Club was organized, the first such club in New England. Up to this time, racing had been for big yachts owned by senior yachtsmen of substantial means and sailed by professional crews. In contrast to this, Burgess and his cronies formed a sort of "Young Turks" movement in the yachting circles of the day. Being well-to-do, they ordered a fleet of catboats from Herreshoff which they campaigned personally up and down the North Shore. When the Eastern Yacht Club was founded at Marblehead in 1871, the sponsors refused to recognize yachts under 25 feet lwl as eligible to enter its races. The result was inevitable. Burgess and his friends formed a new group strictly for small-boat racing and named it the Beverly Yacht Club because the organization meeting had been held in the Beverly home of the Burgess family. Edward Burgess was named as the first commodore.

From 1871 to 1895, Beverly operated without a clubhouse, scheduling regattas in ports convenient to its scattered members, most of whom were enthusiastic young yachtsmen. In this period, races were held anywhere from Marblehead to Marion, Massachusetts, south of Cape Cod.

The first race held at Beverly in June, 1872, included eleven boats in three classes. All but one were catboats, three of them owned by the Burgess boys. The biggest cats were 21-footers, the intermediate, 18-footers, and the smallest, 16-footers. Edward Burgess was in the third or smallest class.

A counterpart race at Toms River, New Jersey, had been held a year earlier. What distinguished the two events was more than geography. Whereas the Beverly Yacht Club event was staged by wealthy young sports, the Toms River event was for working baymen who made their living on the water.

The name Barnegat Bay is often loosely applied to the entire body of water that stretches south from Bay Head, New Jersey, all the way to Cape May. Here a series of shallow estuarine bays lies between the mainland and a string of disconnected offshore barrier islands. Technically, Barnegat Bay is only the northernmost segment of this watercourse, that part between Bay Head and ten miles south of Barnegat Inlet.

The catboat was the standard workboat in this area. Because of the shoals, it was a centerboard boat. Its large carrying capacity and simple rig made it well suited for passage from the mainland to the small settlements such as Chadwicks, Ortley, and the like that were made up of salvagers living off the bay, the sea, and the flotsam washed up on shore. In the spring and fall, these small concentrations attracted well-to-do sports, chiefly from New York, who came for shore-bird shooting on the beach and wildfowling on the Bay.

In 1871 a group of Toms River folk gathered to-

Start of a mixed class of cats and sloops in 1884 off Oregon House, Hull, Massachusetts. (Nathaniel L. Stebbins / Society for the Preservation of New England Antiquities)

gether to form the Toms River Yacht Club. Their first act of business was to raise a purse of $175 and send it with a delegation to Tiffany's in New York City, where they purchased a huge silver cup, thenceforth known as the Toms River Challenge Cup. On July 26, 1871, eight gaff-rigged catboats participated in the first race for the cup. It was won by *Vapor*, owned by Job Falkinburg of Forked River.

The Toms River Challenge Cup is the oldest trophy still competed for by small yachts. Although in some of the early races, sloops were allowed to enter (and occasionally, to win), the race is, and essentially always has been, for catboats.

Catboat racing has continued actively ever since from Bay Head to Cape May and points in between. One consequence of the interest stirred up by the races for the Toms River Challenge Cup was the development of a variety of distinctive catboat types, including the cabin cats designed by Charles Mower — the Marconi-rigged versions — or by Francis Sweisguth, together with a number of scow, dishpan bow, and smaller half-decked varieties. Among the latter, two stand out: the 17-foot Atlantic City cat built in 1913 to a design by Bowes and Mower, and the 15-foot cat-rigged Barnegat Bay sneakbox built by Perrine in the town of Barnegat in the 1920's. This boat in particular became popular for class racing well beyond its native habitat, reaching as far north as Edgartown, Massachusetts.

From 1872 on, small-boat racing grew by leaps and bounds. In this period, boats were frequently

14

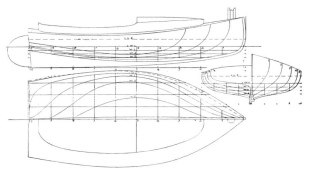

Harbinger's *lines. (W. P. Stephens,* Traditions and Memories of American Yachting.)

Harbinger, *C. C. Hanley's 28' 10" racer of 1889, carried 1551 square feet of sail in a main, jib set on a long, high bowsprit, and a spinnaker. In this shot, she has apparently just broken her spinnaker boom.* Harbinger's *signal victory at Marblehead on July 15, 1889, over two 30-foot cutters, one by Burgess, the other by William Gardner, brought catboats as racers, and C. C. Hanley as a designer, into prominence for the first time. (Nathaniel L. Stebbins / Society for the Preservation of New England Antiquities)*

raced in mixed classes, generally according to overall length, the catboats and sloops being intermingled. Stephens records that the majority of the catboats sailed and raced on Massachusetts Bay, the waters between Cape Cod and Cape Ann, from 1872 to 1880 were Herreshoff boats, many of them cats of the three original Beverly Yacht Club classes.

Two benchmark events foreshadow the next development in the racing catboat. In 1880, the Beverly Yacht Club held its first regatta on Buzzards Bay, staging the event at Monument Beach. In August, 1883, some 176 boats crossed the starting line at Marblehead in a Beverly Yacht Club race. This was to stand as a high-water mark for starters for the next forty years. These two events and the interest they stirred up, undoubtedly led to the development of the huge racing cat sloops that are the pinnacle of catboat racing.

C. C. Hanley, perhaps the greatest of the racing catboat designers, began his career in the early 1880's at Monument Beach when he had just turned thirty. Handy with tools, he rose to the

challenge of building a catboat after seeing them racing at Monument Beach. Hanley was a blacksmith at the time, and was attracted by the action, the sport, and the glitter, as well as the monetary rewards of yacht racing. He began from scratch without the slightest vestige of technical training, but a few years later he was able to build his two great racing cats, the 28'10" *Harbinger* in 1889 and the 26.2' *Almira* in 1890.

Harbinger was the product of a search for greater speed by hull enlargement coupled with the addition of sail area. Built for Joseph R. Hooper of the Hull (Massachusetts) Yacht Club, she was actually a cat sloop. Her 1,551 square feet of sail area — an incredible spread for a catboat — was divided among a main, a huge jib set on a long, hogged bowsprit, and a substantial spinnaker. *Almira,* also a cat sloop, had less, but proportionately large, sail area considering her shorter overall length. From pictures, it would appear that *Almira's* boom was longer than the height of her mast from deckline to truck. In fact, the boom was so long that the very weight of it aft of the boom crutch actually caused it to sag when at anchor.

Harbinger's greatest race came on July 15, 1889, in a competition with two 30-foot cutters that rated well above her. One was *Saracen* of Boston, designed by Edward Burgess of Beverly Yacht Club fame. The other was *Kathleen* of New York, designed by William Gardner. The two men were preeminent in boat design, and the race attracted great interest in both Boston and New York. *Harbinger* won by twenty minutes on a boat-for-boat basis. Overnight, Hanley's name became known to yachtsmen everywhere, and the catboat, as a racer,

Almira *and* Harbinger *racing on Massachusetts Bay, July 4, 1890. Both boats were built by C. C. Hanley.* Almira *was specially built to defeat Har-* binger. Almira *won the race. (Nathaniel L. Stebbins / Society for the Preservation of New England Antiquities)*

C. C. Hanley, 1851-1934, greatest of the builders of racing catboats and master of the rule-of-thumb method of designing a boat by whittling a half-hull model. (Austin H. Waldron / Mrs. Carleton Moody)

Almira, *best known of C. C. Hanley's racing cats. This boat, which was 26' 2" x 25' 4" x 12' x 2' 6", won a great race against* Harbinger *on July 4, 1890. Some 26 years later she made a clean sweep of her class in racing on Massachusetts Bay. Her boom was so long that it sagged aft of the crutch. (Nathaniel L. Stebbins / Society for the Preservation of New England Antiquities)*

Almira reaching. *The length of* Almira's *spinnaker boom exceeds considerably her overall length of 26′ 2″. Carrying 1125 square feet of sail area,* Almira *represents the peak of the effort to crowd sail on a catboat hull to achieve speed. (Nathaniel L. Stebbins / Society for the Preservation of New England Antiquities)*

gained an impetus that was to last to the turn of the century.

The 26.2-foot catboat *Almira* was built in 1890 in order to beat *Harbinger*. In a great race on July 4, 1890, at South Boston, *Almira* won, netting Hanley, her builder and owner at the time, $250. Hanley is said to have considered *Almira* to be the best he ever turned out.

The work of two outstanding marine photographers, N. L. Stebbins of Boston and C. D. Jackson of Marblehead, has provided a graphic record of catboat racing in Massachusetts Bay from the 1880's to 1910. Their extensive collections of marine pictures of this era fortunately have been preserved. At a later date, Winfield M. Thompson, a catboat owner, was a frequent contributor of delightful articles on catboats to *The Rudder* between 1900 and 1912. A skilled photographer, his pictures of the racing cats of that era add interest to his yarns.

One town where catboat racing held sway for twenty years was Mattapoisett, Massachusetts. E. F. R. Wood (*Sailing Days at Mattapoisett 1870-1960,* Reynolds Printing, New Bedford, Mass.,

1961) notes that, beginning in 1876 with an open regatta, catboat racing became an important feature of village life. The men of the town built and sailed their own catboats in heavy competition for substantial stakes. Wagering among the competing crews added a touch of sport. New summer visitors quickly caught the spirit, chartering catboats for the season and engaging their owners as crews.

Open regattas took place in the 1880's at the nearby towns of New Bedford, Marion, and Woods Hole, as well as the more distant ports of Osterville and Martha's Vineyard. This circuit of open races began to disappear in the 1890's. The private clubs began to exclude non-members and do away with cash prizes, as a means of resolving the growing conflict of amateur versus professional racing. Club racing also led to the development of one-design classes and a great expansion of yachting. In the 1899 regatta of the Mattapoisett Yacht Club, there were twenty-three catboats and seventeen sloops, three of them one-design boats of the Herreshoff Fifteen Class. The trend away from catboat racing, once started, was swift. By 1909 only two catboats competed in the Mattapoisett regatta, but there were twenty-nine sloops, half of them one-design boats.

While catboat racing was entering eclipse at Mattapoisett, its was experiencing a surge of renewed interest at New York. Two men sparked the revival. Frank M. Randall of the Atlantic Yacht Club in Brooklyn had long been a devotee of Crosby catboats. He bought his first cat, *Triad,* in the late 1870's and for the next twenty years, is said to have owned from two to eight different catboats a year, mostly built on order by the Crosbys.

Crosby cats have been famous on Cape Cod for 120 years. It took several generations of Crosby builders to develop the sturdy, able fishing cat that is today known as the Cape Cod cat. Many of them were raced informally around the circuit of the Cape and the Islands.

In 1896, Randall persuaded young H. Manley Crosby to move from Osterville to the Bay Ridge section of Brooklyn where the Crosby Catboat and Yacht Building Company was soon turning out catboats. *Step Lively* was a new breed of cat. Long (34′9″), shallow (1′9″ draft), and low with overhangs, she was a distinct departure from her Cape Cod forebears, but she reintroduced catboat racing to New York waters. A whole series of Crosby racing catboats, including *Ethel, Hit or Miss,* and *Presto,* emerged from this beginning and for six or

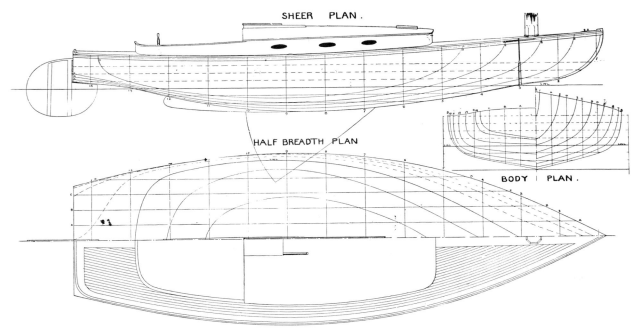

SHEER PLAN.

HALF BREADTH PLAN

BODY PLAN.

ACCOMODATION PLAN

Step Lively represents the extreme development of the racing catboat. She was built in 1896 at Brooklyn, New York, by H. Manley Crosby for Commodore Frank M. Randall of the Atlantic Yacht Club. Randall sparked a revival of catboat racing in New York waters that lasted until 1901. Step Lively was a new breed of cat. Long (34' 9"), shallow (1' 9" draft), and low, with overhangs, reverses at each end of the waterline, and no outside keel or deadwood, she was a distinct departure from her Cape Cod forebears. She finished second in her first race, June 1896, won the next four races in succession, and was leading in the sixth race when she took a wrong turn. Shortly thereafter she was sold. Renamed Dorothy, her subsequent racing career was undistinguished. (The Catbook, 1903, Rudder Publishing Co., N.Y.)*

seven years catboat racing was a lively sport in New York waters. But it didn't last, and in 1900 Crosby packed up and returned to Osterville.

Catboat racing in the first decade of the twentieth century was most actively pursued at the Quincy Yacht Club, where shallow waters encouraged the use of the shoal-draft centerboard cats. According to Winfield M. Thompson, writing in *The Rudder* in 1908, catboats had been raced at Quincy since 1873. Charles Francis Adams II, one of the great yachtsmen of all time, is said to have learned sailing at the helm of a catboat out of Quincy.

In 1904, the Cape Cat Association was organized at Quincy "to keep boats of this type together and make interesting and instructive racing." Some thirty boats or so from various clubs made up the membership of the Association. Donation of the Captain Kidd Plate in the Spring of 1907 as a special prize for catboats stimulated keen competition in a season that ran from May 30 to September 8.

"Maturity of body and mind," Thompson wrote, "distinguished the personnel of the cat racers. The brash youth may go in for new types, changing his love each season. The cat man grows old with his boat and finds her better every year."

Most of the catboats participating in the Quincy races were old-timers, including *Iris*, then nineteen years old, and *Almira*, winner of the 1890 duel with *Harbinger*. *Dartwell*, ex-*Clara*, was a mere youngster, having been built in 1895.

Under rules adopted by the Cape Cat Boat Association, minimum and maximum overall lengths of 22 and 27 feet restricted the racing to the larger cats. Long hogged bowsprits and jibs were permitted. A contemporary reporter observes: "One thing that has been very noticeable about the cats, especially when they have been racing in a strong breeze, is the fallacy of trying to carry too much sail. The boats are generally over-sparred and over-crowded with canvas."

18

H. (for Horace) Manley Crosby, 1871-1959. The picture was probably taken in the years 1896-1901 when Crosby had a boat shop in the Bay Ridge section of Brooklyn, New York. (Osterville Historical Society Collection)

This tendency to drive a catboat in racing perhaps lies behind a commentary often encountered, to the effect that such overcrowding of sail led to accidents and loss of life, thereby bringing the catboat into disfavor and hastening her decline. More than a decade of delving into catboats has produced no authenticated case of death in this manner. However, it has turned up another factor of telling importance. During the last decade of the nineteenth century, many hands were turning to catboat design. In 1903, *The Rudder* published *The Cat Book*, consisting of a dozen catboat designs, many by well-known designers, including V. D. Bacon, H. C. Wintringham, and A. Cary Smith. The results were startling to say the least. The clean, graceful utilitarian lines of the working cat were discarded in favor of long overhangs, reverse curves, and similar aberrations. So extreme were the consequences that steps were taken to eliminate all such alley cats from competition. The Inter-Bay Cabin Catboat Association was organized in 1910 to encourage builders "to produce types of catboats free from all freak features." Design corruption was obviously a more significant factor in

discrediting the catboat than actual loss of life from hard sailing.

The Inter-Bay Cabin Catboat Association was formed by five groups: The Cape Catboat Association of Massachusetts Bay, the Narragansett Bay Yacht Racing Association, the Yacht Racing Association of Southeastern Long Island, the Yacht Racing Association of Barnegat Bay, and the New Bedford Yacht Club. The new Association proposed regional racing for centerboard cabin catboats. Jibs and sails other than the main were barred.

At least two regattas were held under the auspices of this association, one in Massachusetts Bay and the other in Narragansett Bay. This attempt at regional catboat racing faced a special problem. It is one thing to go from Quincy to Marblehead for a race. It is something else to go the long distance from Barnegat Bay in New Jersey to Bristol, Rhode Island, engage in a week of racing, and then return to Barnegat — which is what one unsuccessful entry had to do.

Dolly III, a Daniel Crosby cat built specially for the Second Interbay Catboat match held at Bristol in 1911, nosed out the 20-year-old Hanley cat *Iris* for first place. Since both were entries of the Quincy Yacht Club, the races were automatically returned to Quincy for the 1912 series. Apparently, they never again left there. However, catboat racing in Massachusetts Bay continued almost up to our entry into World War I. *Almira*, in 1916 at age 26, made a clean sweep in her class, finishing one race ahead of an R boat and a Sonder, both fast, sloop-rigged craft. However, this phase of large racing cats in New England waters was drawing to a close. *Almira's* sweeping victory, the war, the lack of new large cats to infuse fresh blood into the thinning ranks, the rise of new and faster types of boats, and the declining interest in the cat as a racer all had a share in the final demise. *The Rudder* for April 1924 carried an ad offering *Almira* with the epitaph: "Price low for quick sale."

Long after catboat racing had disappeared in New England waters, it could be found on Barnegat Bay, where the Barnegat Bay Yacht Racing Association encouraged active competition in the 1920's. Interest revived to such an extent that there was a ready market for rebuilt old Crosby and Hanley boats. Contemporary designs by Mower and Sweisguth produced large, low-headed gaff- and Marconi-rigged affairs. These large cats

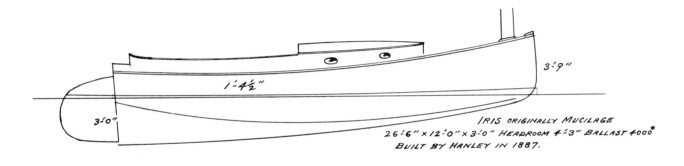

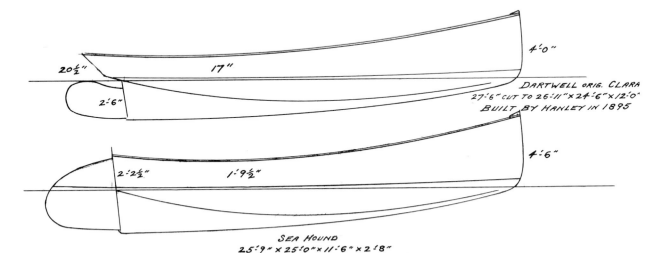

IRIS ORIGINALLY MUCILAGE
26'-6" x 12'-0" x 3'-0" HEADROOM 4'-3" BALLAST 4000*
BUILT BY HANLEY IN 1887.

DARTWELL ORIG. CLARA
27'-6" CUT TO 26'-11" x 24'-6" x 12'-0"
BUILT BY HANLEY IN 1895

SEA HOUND
25'-9" x 25'-0" x 11'-6" x 2'-8"
SAIL AREA 725 ⌀ HEADROOM 5'-4"
BUILT BY CHARLES CROSBY 1911.

Study made by Fenwick C. Williams of the comparative lines of three fast cats. (Fenwick C. Williams)

Iris, ex-Mucilage. *C. C. Hanley's 26' 6" x 12' 0" racing cat of 1887.* Mucilage *cleaned up at Newport, Rhode Island, on July 4, 1888. After years of inactivity, she returned as* Iris *to win the championship of Massachusetts Bay in 1907. (C. D. Jackson / Collection of John M. Leavens)*

20

Clara (later Dartwell); 27' x 11' 6", built by C. C. Hanley in 1895, was an outstanding racer for two decades on Massachusetts Bay. (Nathaniel Stebbins/ Society for the Preservation of New England Antiquities)

Sea Hound, built by Charles Crosby in 1911.

and the smaller Perrine-built, cat-rigged Barnegat sneak boxes provided the new blood that kept cat-boat racing alive well into the early Depression years. After that, catboat racing declined again. However, racing for the Toms River Challenge Cup by the few remaining large cats is still a big event on the Bay.

Elsewhere in this book, the role of the Beetle Cat in racing since 1920 is treated extensively.

Mention should also be made, in passing, of racing in the Taft Cup catboats on the Great Lakes. These special-design craft look more like gaff-rigged sloops sailed without jibs than traditional catboats, but they have raced actively since 1911 for a special trophy contributed by President William Howard Taft. The competition continues to this day.

Sporadic racing in catboats also could be found at scattered places such as Biloxi, Mississippi, where a special breed of cat existed. The Biloxi boats, however, were of local interest only and had little or no influence beyond there.

Wynnsong (left) owned by Commander Alan Thewlis and Victoria (right) owned by Senator James A. Mills, engage in a tacking duel during "The Great Catboat Race," Mission Bay, San Diego, California, July 30, 1972. (Union-Tribune Publishing Co./ Senator James A. Mills)

Cats in flight. Catboats racing in the Saybrook-Duck Island race on Long Island Sound, August 18, 1962. The Catboat Association developed from conversations during the raft that followed this race. Cats (left to right) are: Tang, *two unidentified,* Pinkletink, Chunky, *and* Falcon. *(Foster Nostrand)*

The revival of present-day interest in catboat racing stems from a few informal races in the mid-1950's held by catboat-owning members of the Essex (Connecticut) Yacht Club. The donation, in 1958, by Russell Marston, of a mounted half-hull model as a trophy for a catboat race led to the establishment of an annual open catboat race on Long Island Sound from Saybrook Light to Duck Island. Henry Towers, then commodore of the Essex Yacht Club, and Paul Birdsall were, perhaps, the two leading spirits in making this event a success.

In 1962, at the fifth such race, The Catboat Association emerged. In turn, it has encouraged catboat races at a number of places. The 1972 schedule included regattas at Edgartown, Osterville, Cuttyhunk, Padanarum, and Scituate in Massachusetts; Narragansett Bay, Rhode Island; Saybrook-Duck Island, Connecticut; and Shelter Island and Great Kills, Staten Island, in New York. The latter race marked the resumption of catboat racing in New York City waters for the first time in at least 50 years.

The 18-foot Marshall fiberglass Sanderling, first produced in 1963, has brought a fresh dimension to catboat racing. She has proven to be a relatively inexpensive, very fast, seaworthy boat adaptable to cruising and day sailing, as well as racing. Small fleets of Sanderlings have sprung up in widely separated sections of the country. There are now substantial fleets of racing Sanderlings at Nantucket, the Shrewsbury River, and Atlantic City in New Jersey, the Texas Gulf Coast, and Seattle.

Because of cost factors, few new wood catboats are being built, and the future of catboat racing, therefore, on any grand scale will depend on new and expanded fleets of the less expensive fiberglass cats. However, wood cats are durable, and racing in wood cats, at present levels, will be around for a long time to come.

Chapter 3

CATBOAT DESIGN
by Fenwick C. Williams

Fenwick C. Williams, according to the late John Killam Murphy, who owned five catboats during his 70 years of sailing, has designed more catboats than any living person.

Born in Cambridge, Massachusetts, in December 1901, he joined the staff of John G. Alden as a draftsman in 1923 and, except for a three-year lapse, remained there for 28 years. During this time he designed small yachts and large work vessels. Among his many designs was the catboat Tabby, *Murphy's fourth and best-loved cat.*

Over a period of three years Fenwick Williams set forth the design elements of the catboat, perhaps the most thorough analysis and description of its kind for any small boat. It is from this material that the present chapter has been condensed. Omitted from this condensation are Fenwick Williams papers dealing with:

Measuring area and volume (he observes: "The Catboat is what might be called a relatively noncritical design in that any such form which appears about right to the practical eye is quite likely to come within reasonable limits of displacement, stability and trim.")

Displacement (he notes that in the case of the catboat "no abnormal placement of ballast would be required in order to obtain normal trim.")

Stability (he makes the following observations: "it is quite obvious at a glance that any hull of catboat proportions is going to manifest a strong determination to remain upright under almost anything like normal conditions.")

Balance (he comments: "I don't see that one can do very much about balance in a cat; there is only one place for the mast, the rig looks rather bobtailed if the boom doesn't extend at least to the end of the rudder, the centerboard has to be between the engine and the toilet bowl, with little room to spare, and that seems to be about it. Highly scientific.")

Those interested in the technical details of these papers can consult Fenwick Williams's series "Design Elements of a Catboat" published serially in Bulletins of the Catboat Association.

John M. Leavens

It has sometimes been remarked that what we call the Cape Cod catboat is not merely a boat with a cat rig, but rather a definite combination of hull and rig, and this is certainly very true. Starting out as a workboat for use by men of much less than ample means, the type was well suited to make use of inexpensive and readily available materials.

Ample beam made the use of stone ballast entirely feasible, while the high bow provided good support for the unstayed mast and avoided the necessity for wire standing rigging and attendant fittings. The "barn door" rudder provided adequate strength even when the hull form and the sail plan were such as to produce excessive weather helm. The

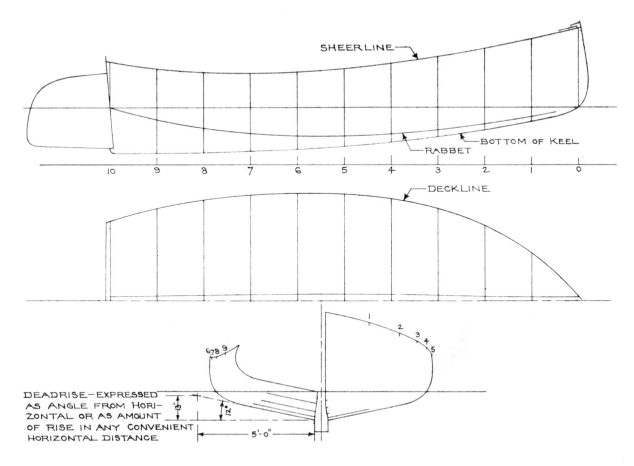

SHEERLINE

BOTTOM OF KEEL

RABBET

DECKLINE

DEADRISE – EXPRESSED
AS ANGLE FROM HORI-
ZONTAL OR AS AMOUNT
OF RISE IN ANY CONVENIENT
HORIZONTAL DISTANCE

5'-0"

Figure 1. Profile, plan view, and body plan of a 20-foot catboat. (Fenwick C. Williams)

high coamings served to keep the water out. The long oval "cat's eye" ports cut less wood across the grain for a given amount of light than did those more nearly round. The relatively low side decks, very low in many of the older boats, provided a handy ledge on which to set a lobster trap, or perhaps an intermediate resting place for a big fish. As the features evolved in the course of time into an always more perfect combination, we ended up with something as completely satisfying in its way as the Cape Cod house.

THE LINES PLAN –
PRELIMINARY CONSIDERATIONS

Let us say that our requirements call for a catboat 20 feet long, which, as always, we desire to make smart in appearance, quite fast, and ex-

tremely able. Since nearly everybody is interested at the outset in how she will look when seen broadside, we will commence with the profile. This is the uppermost drawing in Figure 1. Since snappy appearance is important, the freeboard, or the distance from the waterline to the deck must not be excessive and the sheer must be very "lively." Over the years a few general rules have evolved for guidance in arriving at various and sundry proportions. These rules are not the Law and the Gospels, but, when used with discretion, they do help one to arrive at suitable dimensions.

We will select, for length, a waterline of 20 feet and divide it up nice and even in 10 spaces of 2 feet each. Quite often, for reasons connected more with construction than design, this ten-station spacing is not employed, but we are more concerned with design, and so will do it this way. Now somewhere along this 20-foot line the lowest point of freeboard will be located, and just where is important to the appearance of the above-water profile. Experience indicates that this point should come between two-thirds and three-fourths of the waterline length from the forward end, say on Station 7. Now we'll pull another rule out of the hat and say that the freeboard at the stern can be one and a third times the least freeboard. This curls the sheer up aft somewhat more than is usual, and we may lose our nerve and cut it down a trifle before we get through. Still another rule, also an entirely personal one without any authority, suggests that the bow freeboard can be the sum of the least freeboard and the stern freeboard, or three feet, six inches. A somewhat parabolic line swept through these three points under the control of what we hope is a well trained eye seems to result in the desired "springy" sheer. We now connect the sheer line with the waterline by lines defining the bow and stern profiles. At the stern it is easy; just give the transom a little rake aft so it won't look too severely plumb. But the bow or stem profile can be extremely controversial. Many feel most strongly that any rollback or tumblehome in the stem is utterly hideous and no argument about it. We feel that a fair amount is very much in keeping with the traditions of the type and artistically justified as a factor in tieing the composition together. Putting the foremost point of the stem about one-third of its height above the waterline seems to give the effect we are after, so we draw it in that way.

We now must do something about giving our profile an underbody. The rabbet line, along the garboard seam, where the bottom planking joins the keel, has a fore and aft sweep that is most important. To determine the maximum depth from waterline to rabbet we ought to draw a midship section, but the appearance of things, based on experience, indicates that 15 inches should be about right, so we'll try it. The lowest point of the rabbet line will be about at the maximum section, about halfway between Station 5 and Station 6. We like to see the rabbet line meet the waterline just about at the bottom of the transom, and so it will be drawn. A curved line for the bottom of the keel will just about complete the profile, except for the barn door rudder. Some cats have very little depth of keel below the rabbet, except well aft, but a fair amount of keel adds little to the fixed draft and

actually makes it possible for the boat to gain something to windward in smooth water with the centerboard entirely raised. It also enables us to get by with a somewhat smaller board, an advantage structurally and accommodation-wise. We have settled on a two-foot draft with board up, certainly shoal enough for most sailing areas.

Next comes the matter of how the cat will look in plan view, looking down on the deck. This is shown in the middle drawing in Figure 1. It involves determination of the maximum width, or beam. Catboat practice calls for a beam of slightly less than half the length. With the single large sail, this has been found to give most satisfactory performance. We may as well select 9′ 6″ as our beam, and a transom width of 7′ 0″ seems suitable. Catboat decklines vary considerably. Some are quite sharp forward, with an appearance almost wedge shaped. Our selection is toward the opposite extreme, perhaps a trifle too full just abaft the stem, but we'll let it go for now.

We now lay out the half width of the keel and stem on the plan view. In way of the centerboard trunk there must be width enough for the slot, plus plenty of wood on each side. Seven inches should be adequate. Stem and sternpost can be 4′, with an easy fairing to the wider keel.

Preparation can at this point be made for laying out the body plan, on which the sections appear. This is shown in the bottom drawing of Figure 1. Following the time-honored convention, we show the forebody half sections to the right of the centerline, and the afterbody to the left. By plotting the sheer and deckline, heights and half breadths from centerline and waterline, and drawing a curve through them, we obtain the upper boundary of a view looking from forward aft and from aft forward. In a similar manner the end views of the keel will be shown.

The midship or maximum section, which will actually be a little aft of the mid-length of the waterline, must now be drawn. It could have been drawn as soon as the sheerline and the beam were determined. The rabbet line on the profile was drawn with the idea of providing for a moderate amount of deadrise. On most cats by this designer, the angle of deadrise has come to just about 12°. This gives a hull form which offers excellent performance characteristics and deep enough to be very seaworthy while retaining the initial stability or stability due to form of the beamy, shoal-draft types. If the deadrise were much less, it would be said that she was a "flat-floored" model, and if much more, we aren't certain just what the term would be, "sharp floored" or "steep deadrise," perhaps. Drawing in the turn of the bilge to complete the section, we produce a rather "hard bilge" shape. If the bilge were still "harder," that is with a quicker turn, making it a little wider at the waterline, there would be even more stability, but the frames would be harder to bend and the sides above water would have a rather "wall sided" appearance. Therefore we decided that what is drawn represents a good compromise, and the bilge is hard enough so that in combination with other design features it should make her a regular old sail carrier.

At this point the transom stern can be outlined. We like to make the deadrise angle constant from Station 4 or Station 5 to the stern, so it remains only to connect the deadrise line with the after corner of the sheer and deckline with a curve which shows a bit of tumblehome at the top. This seems to pep up the transom a good deal with an old-time touch.

COMPONENTS OF THE LINES PLAN

A boat form is a solid geometrically in that it has three dimensions: length, breadth, and thickness. In a boat, which is a rather special form of solid, these views, in general, are:

The *profile* with all the lines which appear on it, such as sheer, rabbet, keel, stem, stern, and buttocks.

The *sections,* which take the form of the body plan and which quite clearly are the intersections between the hull surface and a number of transverse, or athwartship, or crosswise vertical planes.

The *plan view,* showing the deckline, waterlines, and half breadth of keel.

The *diagonals,* in one sense, are not necessary for an adequate presentation of the form, yet they are very useful indeed as fairing lines.

The purpose of the lines plan, then, is simply to present the three essential views: profile, sections, and plan view, plus the diagonals.

One can picture a solid as intersected by planes in any number of positions, and the intersections of these planes with the surface of the solid could be drawn on paper. It's all a matter of how you like to cut up your apple, but for boat work the system is pretty well established.

The concept of planes passing through the hull is important, and not at all difficult to grasp. The

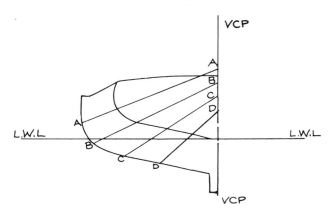

Figure 2. The diagonals. (Fenwick C. Williams)

lines of a boat, for the most part, are the intersections of these planes and the surface of the hull. It has to be kept in mind that most of the straight lines are planes seen on edge. Where waterlines appear as straight lines, they are planes viewed either from side to side or fore and aft. Buttocks are planes which appear as straight lines when viewed directly fore and aft, straight up or down. The diagonals (see Figure 2) also are planes passing through the geometrical solid, but since they are put in obliquely, they appear straight only when viewed directly fore and aft. Thus diagonals A-A, B-B, and C-C seen from this perspective appear as straight lines.

PREPARING THE LINES PLAN

In an attempt to save time, space, and tedium, Figure 3 shows the completed lines drawing. In some ways it might be well to make a separate drawing to illustrate each step or stage involved in the preparation of the lines plan. This would be quite time consuming and tedious. It also would be difficult to do in that most of the steps are not taken in exact sequence one at a time, but are carried out in a sort of overlapping and back-tracking manner. The process is much more difficult to describe than to perform, especially where a good deal of experience makes it relatively easy to achieve the desired result. For example, with the profile, deckline, midship, and stern or transom of our first or outline drawing quite definitely, though not irrevocably, fixed, we would probably sketch in on the plan view a tentative half plan of the waterline plane. Then we would most likely sketch in on the body plan a section about midway between the already-determined midship sec-

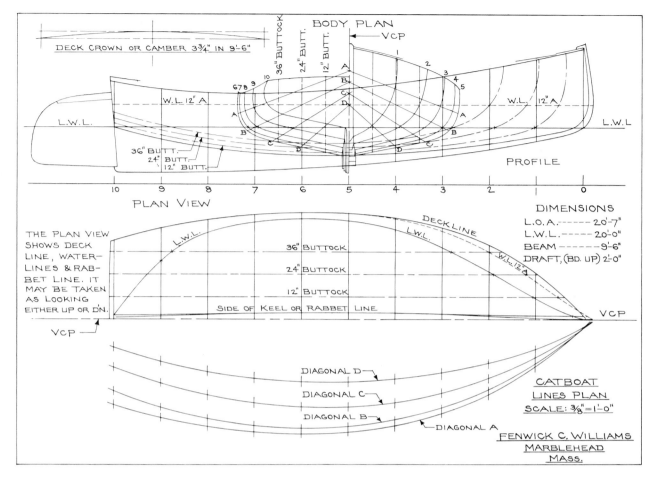

Figure 3. The completed lines drawing of a 20-foot catboat. (Fenwick C. Williams)

tion and the bow, say at Station 3. If a section at this point, which looked about right to us, happened to cross the waterline at the same distance from the centerline as the waterline on the plan view, well and good; otherwise it becomes necessary either to alter the waterline in the plan view or to alter the section, and so it goes for each element which has to agree with every other.

The Waterline All boatmen are familiar with half models, usually mounted on a board. By referring alternately to a supposed model or half model and to the lines drawing, things can perhaps be made clear somewhat more quickly. At the very beginning, we established a waterline as a line of reference above which to draw the above-water profile and below which to determine the fore and aft curvature of the underbody.

In drawing the waterline on the plan view, it will be seen that the midship section gives the half breadth of the waterline at the point where this section is drawn, and at the stern, as the outline of the transom shows, the waterline comes in to the sternpost, or to the after end of the rabbet line, which amounts to the same thing. From the forward end of the waterline at Station 0, through the point of greatest width at or near the midship section and back to the stern, we draw this waterline curve, guided by three points only, plus any judgment which may come to bear. Since any number of curves can be drawn through three points, the matter of judgment is fairly important. Once we have an intermediate section established, as at Station 3, we have a fourth control point on our waterline curve, and the possible variations in

27

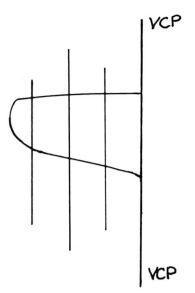

VCP

VCP

Figure 4. The buttock lines. (Fenwick C. Williams)

the curve become very much more restricted. Thus by trial and error, alterations and compromise, things are gradually pulled together into something definite.

Actually, in this particular design, where we have made the lower, or deadrise portion of all the sections from amidships aft exactly parallel, the shape of the waterline in this area is quite definitely determined and the whole thing is duck soup. It is a lazy man's design aft of amidships; why not, since there is some reason to believe that it may well be the best form we could give it?

A great deal could be written about this waterline, which, of course, represents the surface of smooth water, the plane of flotation. It is usually designated LWL for load waterline, the waterline at which the boat is supposed to float when normally loaded. It can also be called the DWL for designed waterline, and the same letters can be taken to mean datum waterline, or the waterline on which measurements are based and from which assorted items of mathematical information are obtained. We are inclined to favor the latter designation as sounding impressively scientific without promising too much in exactness of flotation line. Anyhow, this all-important line in its horizontal plane is the intersection of the hull surface and the surface of smooth water with the boat floating at this level.

The Buttock Lines The buttocks are simply the

curves you would get if a model were sawed through, fore and aft, in planes perpendicular to the waterline and parallel to the fore and aft centerline. (See Figure 4).

The contact surface between any half-hull model and the board on which it is mounted is the longitudinal vertical centerline plane, the same plane that would be used to make a full model into a half model. Now suppose we were to saw our model through lengthwise in one, two, or more perfectly straight, flat cuts exactly parallel with the vertical centerline plane and at any convenient or desired distance from it. The edges of the lengthwise sections thus obtained would be the buttock lines of the model and of the lines drawing. The model could very well be made up of similar pieces glued together, and the glue joints would then be these same buttocks lines. Since we may have to refer to the longitudinal vertical centerline plane a number of times, we may as well use the initials VCP and omit the letter for longitudinal, it being understood that all the planes we are concerned with are longitudinal except the sections.

The Diagonals Having tried to make somewhat clear the nature and function of the sections, waterlines, and buttocks, we come now to the fourth set of planes, which is also the third set of longitudinal planes, that whose intersection with the hull surface forms the group of curves known as the diagonals. These are not suitable for model work because, while a model could conceivably be made up on the diagonal planes, it would involve the use of wedge-shaped pieces, which would be difficult to shape accurately or to peg or glue together in a satisfactory manner. Diagonals, doubtless came in with the draftsmen, but they provide a very useful system of supplementary fairing lines. The only intersection between planes we need to be concerned with is that between each diagonal plane and the VCP. Perhaps it will help to picture each diagonal plane as a perfectly flat, infinitely thin plate which is hinged to the VCP at a suitably selected height which, in the case of a shoal-draft boat, is usually above the LWL. This hinge line is made parallel with the LWL, and so, when viewed end-on, the diagonal planes appear as straight lines in the body plan, seen as A-A, B-B, etc. (see Figure 3). Picturing these planes as free to hinge up or down from the hinge line, it can be seen that, if swung into a horizontal position, they will coincide with, or at least be parallel with, some of the waterline planes, while if allowed to

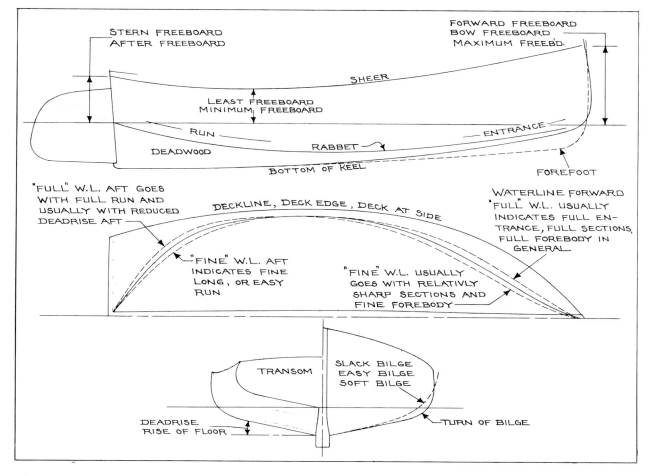

Figure 5. Typical terms used in boat design. (Fenwick C. Williams)

drop straight down they would all coincide with the VCP. Our object, in order to make these planes useful to us, is to swing them into such a position that, as nearly as practicable, they will be at right angles to the sections. If a fair curve misses some of the points on a given diagonal, the sections corresponding to such missed points have to be adjusted. It isn't quite as bad at it may appear, although sometimes a bit troublesome.

HALF HULLS VS LINES DRAWINGS

Probably most half models are made in separate pieces above and below the waterline plane, so that the line of meeting, whether separable or glued, will show the shape of the waterline. The model could, in addition, be made in a number of horizontal layers of any convenient thickness, glued or pegged together, the pegging method having

been used until the advent of the drafting system in order to obtain the shape of the model for enlargement to the full size of the craft which is to be built.

Shaping a hull by making a model, as compared with drawing it on paper, has both advantages and disadvantages. With a model, one can see more exactly how the finished hull will look, but even in that there are pitfalls, for a model, especially if of small size, can be disproportionately bulky, excessive in depth and high in freeboard, and still look quite attractive. Also a model can, in general, only be made up in one set of parallel layers without becoming a rather hopeless collection of small pieces, whereas on paper, by simple principles of descriptive solid geometry, we can pass as many imaginary planes through our hull as we please, and the intersections of such planes and the hull surface will be curves of various characteristic shapes, which can be observed critically and measured accurately.

NOMENCLATURE AND TERMINOLOGY

Some of the more typical terms used in boat design are illustrated in Figure 5. In general we can begin by calling the 20-foot catboat we have been describing a quite typical present-day catboat with moderate deadrise and a hard, or at least firm bilge, the deadrise being maintained at a constant angle from amidships to the stern, resulting in well-lifted quarters which, in combination with fairly full forward sections, should prevent any marked tendency to depress the bow when heeled.

The above-water profile aims to produce a pleasing sheer, a generally characteristic stem outline, and the usual slightly raked transom on which is hung a barn door rudder of generous size and effective shape.

The underwater profile shows a nearly complete absence of forefoot, as is usual today and has been for some time past. This cutaway forefoot results in U-shaped forward sections, unless the waterline is extremely fine forward, sections which tend to prevent diving into a head chop. This shallow forebody, with consequent lack of forefoot, also makes a boat quicker in stays, as there is less resistance to pivoting about the centerboard. Since this general type of forebody has become virtually standard for catboats, it seems fairly safe to assume that it is the best for cat-rigged craft of shoal draft.

The term *deadrise* appears to be a puzzler to many, but it has been defined as the angle or departure from the horizontal, or the steepness of the bottom portion of the midship and maybe many other sections. Some may wonder how the term originated, and in the absence of definite knowledge one may assume that, as with so many other words, it comes from the terminology of larger craft. The bottom members of heavy, sawn frames were called floors, and a flat, horizontal surface was often called rise of floor above the dead flat. We know it was called rise of floor, and then deadrise.

While speculating as to origins of terms, let's take a crack at *freeboard* and hazard a guess that it referred to the number of boards, or planks, in a vessel's side which stood free of the water.

While the term *bilge* in general refers to the entire bottom portion of a craft's interior, the tendency is to apply the word to the turn of the bilge, where the bottom turns up to the side. In the broader sense, bilge acquired a bad name from the old-time practice of dumping every sort of unsavory material therein and accepting the resulting aroma as inseparable from seagoing life.

Several words are used to indicate the quickness of the turn of the bilge. A chine boat might be said to have a completely hard bilge, since there is an actual angle between the bottom and side. At the opposite extreme is the Block Island double-ender with a bilge so soft, so slack, so easy, as to be almost no bilge at all. In between these extremes lie all degrees of very hard, hard, firm, moderate, and so on to the Block Island type.

In general, a hard bilge is conducive to stiffness and consequent ability to carry sail, but other factors have to be considered, such as beam and location of ballast, as well as amount of ballast.

Mention is made of well-lifted *quarters*, and here we come to a dilemma that is likely to stay with us to the end. The quarters are where you'd expect them to be, the parts that are bumped by a quartering sea. The quarters blend downward to a hard-to-define area known as the *run*, an inexact term, which perhaps can be considered to apply to that portion of the hull along which the water passes in leaving the hull surface. It appears not to be much distinguishable from the afterbody.

The *entrance*, be it fine or full, is the forward portion of the forebody, the portion that parts the water and starts it on its way along the balance of the forebody to the area of maximum acceleration over the bulge of the middlebody and on to a region of diminishing velocity of laminar flow along the afterbody and the run. Figure 5 appears well enough to illustrate fine and full forward and after waterlines with accompanying fineness and fullness of entrance, forebody, afterbody, and run.

In a catboat, the *rabbet*, where the bottom planking meets the keel, is very much a design as well as a structural feature, since there is a definite angle along that line. In a deep-keel boat of the type, say, of a twelve-meter sloop, where the sections are all smooth curves from deck edge to keel bottom, the rabbet line, where the garboard plank is rabbeted into the wood keel, stem, etc., is there all right, but is probably quite invisible when the hull is all slicked up and coated with costly bottom paint.

The *deadwood* area may also be called the skeg, although one thinks of skeg as applying more to a piece attached to the bottom aft as on a skiff. Presumably deadwood refers to filler pieces of limited structural significance that are put in between the keel and other important structural members.

CATBOAT TYPES

The jib-headed or marconi rig is often seen on cat-rigged boats, but this rig can hardly be considered suitable on the typical plumb-stem catboat hull, where the mast is so far forward as to provide little spread for shrouds. Sometimes the mast is set considerably aft so that it can be stayed, and also so that better balance can be achieved with the triangular sail, but then the boat looks more like a sloop minus the jib, and in many cases probably acts that way. Cats specifically designed for the rig, with a fair amount of forward overhang, as with the Barnegat Bay racing cats, appear to be quite satisfactory, but for maximum safety in a cruising boat, it is doubtful if one could conscientiously approve of a lofty mast in a shoal-draft boat with inside ballast.

Very likely, the earliest type of gaff sail used in this country on a cat-rigged boat is, as L. Francis Herreshoff suggests, that which shows a marked Dutch influence, as on the "Point boats" of Newport, Rhode Island. Such a sail is characterized by a long luff secured to the mast by hoops or lacing line, and a short head lashed to a gaff, which in purely Dutch types would be curved and in the more American style generally straight. The foot, of moderate length, would be extended by the boom, but under the more European influence it would be loose footed on the boom, that is, secured only at tack and clew. Increasing Americanization would result in lacing the foot to the boom. Sketch A in Figure 6 shows the loose-footed type. Sails of this general shape were quite apt to have a single halyard for throat and peak. While the ability to control throat and peak separately would seem to be quite an advantage, it is said that the single halyard, when rove off by one who knows how, can work very well.

Sketch B in Figure 6 may be taken as fairly typical of what may be called the first full Americanization of the gaff sail. It would seem to have practically all the disadvantages of every other form, without offering much in compensation. It may be realized that such a "flat-headed" or "square-headed" sail, with little height of mast above the gaff jaws (some examples were more extreme than the one shown), involves a peak halyard which hauls the gaff more strongly against the mast than it hauls up the peak, thus putting a con-

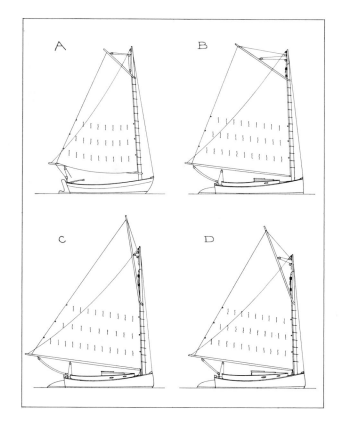

Figure 6. Four catboat types. (Fenwick C. Williams)

siderable compression load on the gaff and a severe bending stress on the mast at the jaws, requiring that nearly the maximum mast diameter be carried up to this point. Very likely such rigs had much to do with giving the cat the bad reputation of being suited only to smooth-water sailing.

It seems certain that every degree of variation between the shapes illustrated has been used somewhere, at sometime, on some boat, and most likely on many boats in numerous localities. To go now to an opposite extreme, Sketch C in Figure 6 shows the development of five or six decades ago in the Massachusetts Bay Cape Catboat Association, which sponsored very strenuous racing in the Boston and Marblehead areas, the fleet consisting largely of 26- and 27-footers, such as *Iris* and *Dartwell* from the Hanley shop and *Dolly III* from Osterville. This is the most "modern" of gaff rigs in that it most closely approaches the marconi. In this small sketch, halyards and sheet are over-simplified, for with these big rigs more parts were needed. One may wonder why, if this is the nearest approach to

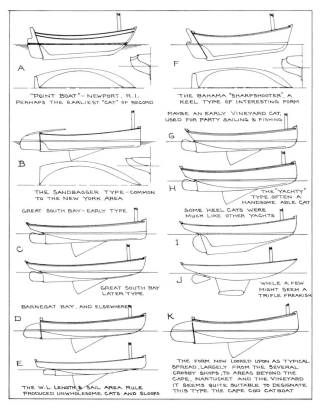

Figure 7. Twelve variations of catboats. (Fenwick C. Williams)

the marconi that the gaff rig has attained, it has for the most part given way to the moderately peaked sail of Sketch D in Figure 6. Our own feeling is that the latter is just more practical in several ways. There is more room for the throat halyard blocks, the gaff jaws are easier to fit, and if it appears that the set of the sail could be improved by further "peaking up," there is space allowed for it.

In the broadest sense, presumably any boat rigged with a mast stepped well forward and a single fore-and-aft sail is a catboat, but those types in which the hull appears to be especially modelled or designed to take the rig always seem to be catboats in a truer sense. In Figure 7 an attempt is made to outline a mere dozen variations of catboats with brief descriptive captions of each.

THE CAT RIG

Figure 8 illustrates the elements of a cat rig. The first step in designing a rig for the 20-foot-waterline boat is to decide on the height of the cabin

trunk in order to see how high the boom will have to be. Modern practice calls for more crown to the trunk or house top than on earlier boats, as that seems to be the least objectionable way in which to gain a little much-desired headroom. This results in cocking up the boom considerably more at the after end than heretofore; a very good thing indeed, since it largely obviates the risk of cracked heads in the cockpit and also greatly reduces the danger of the boom "tripping" in the water as the boat rolls in a quartering sea.

Now it's about time to do something about that important item, the mast. The diameter, we feel, can best be determined by a rough rule based on what has been found to be good practice over a long period of time. A diameter at the deck of eight-tenths of an inch for each foot of beam seems to give a reasonable figure. Since the beam is $9\frac{1}{2}$ feet, we come out with a good, strong $7\frac{1}{2}$ inches as our "rule" mast diameter. To locate this on the profile, it appears that, if the after portion of the mast comes on Station 1 at the deck, it will look about right, and $3\frac{3}{4}$ inches forward of this will be the centerline of the mast.

Some folks claim that a catboat mast should stand quite plumb, but we feel that a little rake, say two degrees, looks a bit livelier, and so we can draw the centerline upward at this angle.

We must have an idea of the sail area which may be found suitable, and since even catboat men understandably are not especially fond of reefing, and today almost invariably have some form of auxiliary power at hand, modern usage calls for considerably less sail than that used in the past. Another rough rule obtained from practice says that an area of 80 percent of the square of the length will give quite good results. Now 80 percent of the square of the waterline length is 320 square feet, and of the overall length 336 square feet. Almost anywhere between the two should do.

From experience in drawing quite a number of similar plans, we have a fairly good idea of what dimensions will give somewhere near the desired area, and we may as well enhance the fun by indulging a personal predilection for even measurement and exact proportion where not incommensurate with the desired result. We may set up a luff measurement of 60 percent of the waterline for a starter. A foot measurement of waterline length plus one foot puts the clew over the end of the rudder, which brings it about as nearly within reach as it can be without looking somewhat docked. It so happens that with the foot angle about as shown, and a head dimension of 1½ times the luff, the leech can equal the luff plus the head. Remarkable. The resulting sail seems to present a reasonable appearance, so we may try it for area by dividing it into two triangles by means of the diagonal, which scales 22′ 4″ and is a useful measurement for the sailmaker. For fear of insulting the reader's mathematical aptitude, we hate to mention the fact that the triangle areas can be found by measuring the altitude from whichever side offers the easiest figuring. To obtain the area (half the product of base and altitude) of the upper triangle, we can measure the perpendicular distance from leech to throat with a half-inch scale to give half the length, or 6.67 and multiply by the chosen base, in this case the leech, 30, and we have 200 square feet, very nearly. For the lower triangle, it seems convenient to multiply half the luff by the perpendicular distance to the clew, or 6 × 20.66 = 124. So, adding the two together, we have an area of 324 square feet, which is within the established limits.

Someone may want to find the center of area, somewhat erroneously called the center of effort, since the actual center of effort moves about in an undetermined manner with every change in shape or setting of the sail. This center is of no real importance, as the sail is of a shape we find pleasing and consider suitable, there is only one location for the sail, and nobody knows where the center ought to be anyhow. However, the medians of a triangle are concurrent at the center of area, and the combined center can be located somewhere on the line joining them by means of graphic proportion, if that is a proper term. Just draw at each triangle center a perpendicular to the line joining them, heading oppositely, and on each perpendicular, from each triangle center, on any convenient scale, lay off a distance representing the area of the opposite triangle. On this plan, using a ¾″ scale and dividing by ten to keep the distance down, a length of 2 was laid off from the center of the lower triangle, and a distance of 1.24 was measured from the center of the upper triangle. Where the straight line joining these points crosses the line joining the triangle centers is the center of the whole, which is the center of area.

Somewhere a piece back we left the mast quite unfinished, and as yet we have no boom or gaff. The length of the mast may be decided by locating the upper peak halyard block just slightly above a

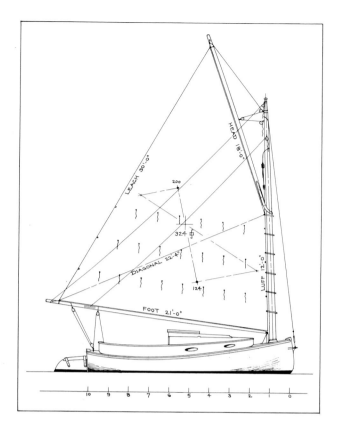

Figure 8. Elements of a cat rig. (Fenwick C. Williams)

point opposite the midlength of the gaff and then adding enough masthead so the topping lift block will stand clear. Mast diameter at the upper halyard block may be a little less than half the diameter at the deck. It is quite traditional for the mast to be hexagonal or octagonal from the keel to slightly above the deck, and this allows the use of flat-faced wedges. Plenty of "drift" for the throat halyard seems a good idea, as it minimizes any twisting stress as the gaff swings off. There is plenty of space with a short luff, so why jam things up? It is nice to have bands for the peak halyard blocks, but they may be hard to obtain and eyebolts are frequently used. Some say they work loose and damage the mast, but in one case at least they have given no trouble in twenty years.

Boom and gaff dimensions can best be found by experience or by reference to similar boats. Probably about half the mast diameter is ample for the boom, with a suitable taper to each end. A pear-shaped gaff section with a groove to take the head of the sail gives good fore and aft or up and down

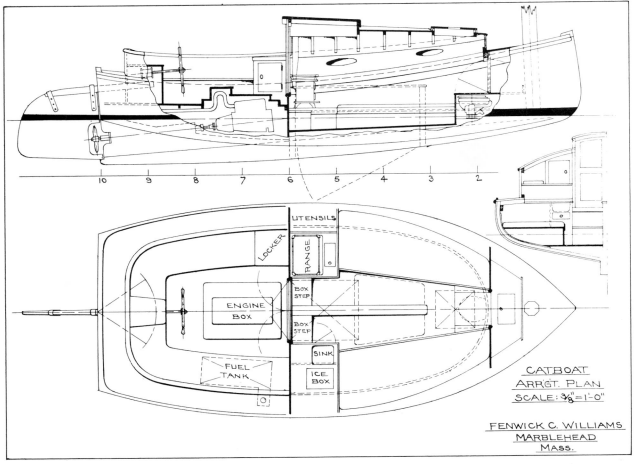

Figure 9. *Cabin and cockpit layout for a 20-foot catboat. (Fenwick C. Williams)*

strength for the weight. A gaff has been known to break from being too light, and there have been complaints of undue weight. There may be some way of getting it right.

Blocks with bridle fittings to run on wire gaff bridles appear to have been discontinued by the manufacturers as of no further interest to the progressive yachtsman. Probably the same weight put into a little extra spruce will produce a gaff that is amply strong without a bridle, so we may as well try it.

Many mast hoops hold a luff straight, but they pile up when sail is lowered and are a chore to lash on, come spring. A spacing of two feet may be a good compromise. The throat cringle is a little hard to secure in the best position on a high-peaked gaff, so a hoop is shown at that point. This may, or may not be a good idea.

A tripod, or "crab" for the boom is traditional, avoids a large, expensive gooseneck band, and also avoids the danger of crushing the vital outer fibers of the mast. It is not difficult to shape a modified version of the old forged iron crabs from a brass strip.

Since, except for a throat halyard block sling, there is only a headstay of wire, we may treat the boat to a good, stout one of stainless steel, either 1/4" diameter, or one size less.

Because we like traditional fittings, and those who don't can leave them off, a combination mooring eye and headstay fitting is shown some distance down from the stemhead.

For running rigging it makes some sense to have everything the same size. Those lines which take the most strain have, or certainly should have, the most parts. The sheet, when hard on the wind in a breeze, may carry four times the load of a topping lift, but if the sheet has four parts, the load per part may be about the same. Three-eighths-inch diameter is ample for strength, and about as small as the hands will tolerate for hauling. This calls for 3″ blocks in wood (1″ shell size for each ⅛″ of rope diameter) or No. 1 bronze blocks. If you want to treat the boat to ash or lignum-vitae blocks for sheet and halyards, or sheet only and the rest bronze, it is quite all right.

Having inadvertently involved an owner in a $55.00 charge for a bronze boom bail, we are inclined to hang the sheet blocks on strops of dacron, or of wire served with marline. The easiest and least expensive way of doing something will often prove entirely safe if one just remembers that it may not last as long and therefore should be examined fairly often, and renewed when doubtful.

Two quarter lifts and a topping lift are indicated, a sort of belt plus suspenders proposition, but having seen one catboat owner nearly knocked out by the boom descending on his dome of thought, we like to provide plenty of means for holding the boom up. The quarter lifts provide for one lift always to windward for topping up when under way. Quarter lifts can be made into lazyjacks by dropping lines from them to the boom, but so long as some adequate lift is provided, the rest is quite optional.

The general preference today is probably for sail track on the boom, and this is all right, although we would have a lacing, since any metal work is apt to be hard on the fingers when reefing.

CABIN AND COCKPIT ARRANGEMENT

Since matters of layout are so subject to considerations of personal requirement and taste, cabin and cockpit arrangements present a problem which can be tackled only with much diffidence and misgiving. Some suggested arrangements are shown in Figure 9.

A few remarks on power may be in order to begin with, since the choice of an engine may to some extent determine the location of the cabin bulkhead. It would be real good fun to have in a boat like this one of the single- or twin-cylinder two-cycle engines that are still produced in Nova Scotia, but since nearly everybody demands clutch, reverse gear, and electric starter, there is probably little use in giving the matter more than passing thought. It appears now that diesel is the coming thing. In fact, small gasoline engines seem to be nearing extinction in this country, except for outboards.

Mention of outboards suggests the probability that an outboard of about ten horsepower would shove this boat along at five knots or so. Such a power plant would save much in machinery and installation costs, eliminate the need for a large hatch in the cockpit, and leave more room for stowage. But here again, the majority, though perhaps not such a large majority, will prefer the convenience and presumably instant availability of inboard power.

Absence of propeller drag can be brought up as a point in favor of outboard power. Few seem to realize the extent to which the resistance of a three-blade, nonfeathering wheel can take the fine edge from the sailing and handling qualities of a boat.

Regardless, however, of all arguments pro and con, an engine installation should be allowed for in the general case, and a hypothetical machine may be drawn in outline of sufficient size to cover anything which could reasonably be called for.

An engine without ample access thereto seems a quite hopeless proposition, so our tendency is to sacrifice uncluttered floor space to whatever hatch arrangement will give the desired working space. Since a really watertight flush hatch is expensive and all but impossible to achieve, a low, raised hatch is fitted over the large opening, a smaller hatch mounted on the bigger one to cover the engine block, and a third housing, no less, sheltering the exhaust loop. This seems complicated, and it is, but in practice works out quite well.

The time-honored quadrant and pinion gear has served well in catboats for many years, but it is a rather short-radius rig which puts a fairly heavy strain on all parts concerned and has quite a lot to say while doing so. Also, costs are ever rising, and on the whole we are inclined to make up a long radius, low stress arrangement using a drum on the wheel shaft, large sheaves outboard, and a large plywood quadrant or just plain abbreviated tiller to which flexible wire is attached.

The matter of tanks has also to be considered in connection with the cockpit. From tanks installed above deck, leakage could drain out through the scuppers, and a side deck fill could be arranged as indicated by means of an outboard extension of the tank, which would also permit simple and direct sounding of the tank. Maybe someone will come along and say that this is quite illegal, but at this writing no reason for such judgment comes to

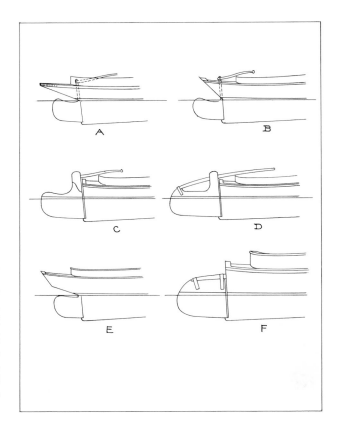

(A) Underslung rudder of the fantail-stern, tiller-steered catboat Metis *built in the 1870s. The wooden rudder stock passes through the hull in a wooden trunk and attaches to a wooden blade. Later, for added strength, iron was used for both tiller and stock, and brass or iron pipe was used for the trunk. (B) Raked-transom cats also used underslung rudders. (C) Old-time cats often had outboard rudders, either one piece, as shown, or two piece, with a separate blade attached to a heavy wooden rudder post. (D) Added strength was obtained by extending the tiller to engage the rudder. (E) Inboard rudder of the style often found on short-overhang cats built as yachts. (F) Classic "barn-door" rudder. The forward end of a short, heavy, wood tiller, held to the blade by metal straps, fits into a geared metal quadrant turned by a steering wheel. (Fenwick C. Williams)*

mind. Leakage, however unlikely, in tanks installed below would be hard to locate and probably impossible to stop, while removal for repair would mean taking out the engine, with attendant grief and cost.

A water tank or tanks may be installed under a cockpit seat, beneath the floor, or under the bunks, but what could be simpler or less expensive than the square-section plastic jugs that sweet cider comes in along about Thanksgiving time?

Having somewhat arranged the outdoor portion, let's see what we can do below. Prospective owners, especially when not very familiar with scale drawings, often feel that it should be possible to effect the best arrangement by trying and fitting in the boat as work progresses. 'Taint so, and every assurance can be given that a better job will result from working things out on paper. Now and then one sees a cabin in which it appears that the various fitments have been tossed in from some distance, and without very good aim. This effect can be avoided with careful planning.

Our own choice of layout is perhaps quite conventional; not very imaginative, but there are rather definite limitations in a small boat. A galley against the bulkhead allows for that supreme comfort, a solid fuel stove of the Shipmate type. Those who cruise in warmer climes may not agree, and a liquid fuel stove, if deemed adequate, can be set a little higher with a convenient locker beneath. Gas also may be used, but it is difficult to extinguish a fire while being propelled through the air by the force of an explosion.

Outboard of the stove there is room under the side deck for a sort of bin for cooking utensils. This could be enclosed, as a locker, if preferred. A solid-fuel stove is customarily built with the fire box on the left side, so it is advisable to locate the stove in the port side of the galley where it faces forward.

On the starboard side the usual thing is to arrange a sink and an ice box. A plastic dishpan which can be emptied into a bucket would be simple and trouble-free, but there are those who would prefer plumbing. A companion hatch of generous size helps the headroom situation considerably and allows for entrance on either side of the centerboard trunk. Companionway doors are a problem. Perhaps for this job, drop slides are best. For companion steps, boxes with hinged or removable treads provide convenient storage for tools, stove fuel, etc.

We come now to the bunks, where a length of 6 foot five or six inches brings us conveniently to the deck beam at the forward end of the house, where can be located a bulkhead on which clock, barometer, bookshelf, and/or radio may be arranged to suit the taste or as space permits.

Bunks have to be quite low because of headroom limits, and the available width at various stations for the selected height is found from the body plan sections with allowance for thickness of planking, frames, and ceiling, or sheathing, a perhaps more meaningful term at present.

There seems to be one obvious place for the toilet, and if its location appears too obvious, a measure of privacy can be had by hanging a curtain across the cabin about at the forward end of the centerboard trunk.

If a platform at the level of the cover of the toilet housing were extended from the bulkhead to the mast, it would serve as a good stowage area for luggage, while the space beneath, although good for general stowage, might contain a septic tank in areas where such are, or may soon be, required. While the behemoths of pollution befoul the waters by the billions of gallons, the yachtsman is picked on for his puny contribution to impurity.

However, in fairness, it has to be admitted that even now there are places where inhabited boats congregated in marinas produce an atmosphere somewhat lacking in delicate fragrance.

A hatch on the forward portion of the cabin trunk will greatly improve ventilation, admit more light if suitably fitted with translucent material, and provide more headroom over the toilet. An expensive plastic trap ventilator may be fittted on the hatch, and this will squash down nicely if the boom is lowered onto it.

The usual hinged table leaf will be fitted on each side of the centerboard trunk. The height of the trunk is not critical, and in many cases it can be made to suit the table height, which is critical. Ten inches from the top of the bunk cushion to the table usually seems about right.

Back to the cockpit, but continuing the ventilation theme, we have to meet the Coast Guard requirements applying to gasoline-powered boats. An electric blower for exhausting fumes is viewed with favor. Much air has to be admitted anyway, as an operating engine inhales a great deal in the process of producing hot vapors and power, and it has to come from the general atmospheric supply, however polluted. Air ducts from the bilge are, of course, a feature of present requirements.

Chapter 4

HOW I TOOK OFF PINKLETINK'S LINES
by Edson Irwin Shock

For some years I had wanted to have Pinkletink's *lines taken off but the process always seemed arcane and mysterious. Then one day Ed Schock mentioned casually that, since his retirement from the faculty of the University of Rhode Island, he had been engaged by the Marine Historical Association to take off lines and to make lines drawings and half hull models of boats in the Mystic Seaport collection.*

On Friday, July 28, 1967, by prearrangement, we had Pinkletink *hauled at the Ram Point Marina in Wakefield, Rhode Island, and Ed Schock went to work on her. The result is a set of* Pinkletink's *lines.*

Ed Schock's interesting narrative describes how he did it.

John M. Leavens

With the boat in the water, and no one aboard, the freeboard was measured at the bow, stern, and six other points along the sheer. This established the sheer line. The boat was then hauled out on a trailer, which was parked on a level spot, allowing room to work on one side of the hull.

As Figure 10 shows, a baseline was made, parallel to the center of the boat, by stretching a string between two spikes driven into the ground, a distance A out from the center. The distance A was measured at right angles to the keel centerline, which is always difficult to do. The way it was done was to establish points x and z with a plumb bob and an arc was drawn with a radius of A from each of the points x and z. The baseline string was then stretched tangent to the arcs.

A surveyor's transit was set up at each of the points along the baseline (1, 2, 3, 4, etc. in Figure 10), and the distance from the forward end of the baseline was measured at each point. These points were spaced so as to be close together where the

shape of the hull changes rapidly as it does at the ends, and farther apart where the lines sweep gently. The instrument was set over the baselines, and the distance B was measured. Measurement from point to point accumulates errors, but if each point is located from the zero point, one wrong measurement does not affect the others.

The instrument was leveled and the horizontal scale was set at zero. A sight was taken first on one end of the baseline. Then the transit was turned 90 degrees of horizontal angle to get the line of sight at right angles to the centerline of the boat. (See Figure 11).

Next, sights were taken on various points of the hull, and the angle from the horizontal to the points was measured using the vertical scale on the transit. The distance from each point to the center of the horizontal axis of the telescope was measured and recorded. In Figure 11, point 1 is at the sheer, while point 2 is any point between the sheer and the horizontal, and point 3 is horizontal-

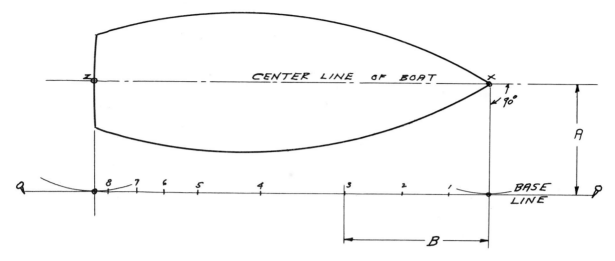

Figure 10. Setting the base line. (Edson Irwin Schock)

Edson I. Schock taking off Pinkletink's *lines. (John M. Leavens)*

Figure 11. Getting a line of sight at right angles. (Edson Irwin Schock)

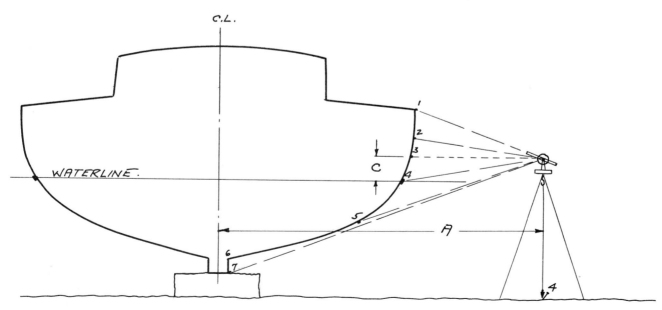

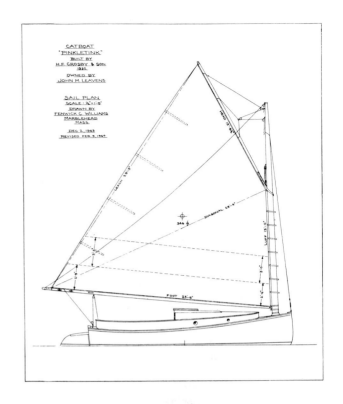

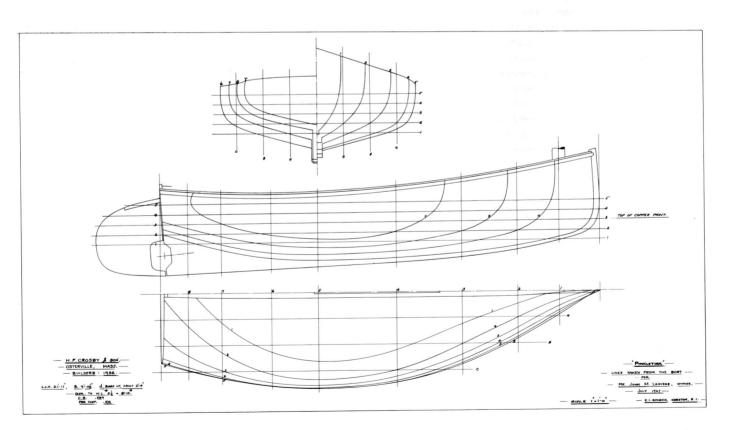

40

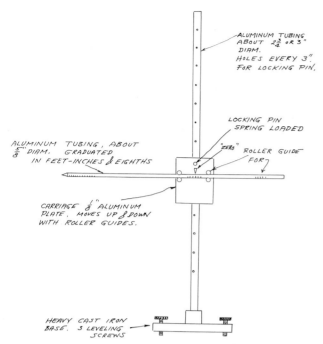

ALUMINUM TUBING
ABOUT 2¾ OR 3"
DIAM.
HOLES EVERY 3"
FOR LOCKING PIN,

ALUMINUM TUBING, ABOUT
⅝" DIAM, GRADUATED
IN FEET-INCHES & EIGHTHS

LOCKING PIN
SPRING LOADED

"ZERO" ROLLER GUIDE
FOR

CARRIAGE ⅜" ALUMINUM
PLATE, MOVES UP & DOWN
WITH ROLLER GUIDES.

HEAVY CAST IRON
BASE. 3 LEVELING
SCREWS

Figure 12. Apparatus for taking off lines on a level floor. (Edson Irwin Schock)

ly opposite the center of the telescope. This horizontal point opposite the telescope was taken on each station, and the distance from it to the waterline, *C*, was measured. This is important because it establishes the height of the transit from the waterline. The dirty mark on the hull where the boat floats is used for the waterline. If she has recently been scrubbed, and the hull shows no such mark, you have to use the line of the copper paint and hope it is straight.

More points than considered necessary were taken. When drawing the section it is good to have a few extra points to get the exact curve of the section. A point 6 on the rabbet, and a point 7 on the bottom of the keel were obtained.

One measurer held the end of the tape against the boat, and the other measurer located the point and read off the distance from the tape at the instrument end, and also read off the vertical angle for the point. A third person recorded the data as read. At each point the vertical angle and distance is needed. The instrument also must be located at each station setting along the baseline for distances *A* (Figure 11), *B* (Figure 10), and *C* (Figure 11).

Figure 11 shows the transit set up over station 4. Point 6 on the rabbet line is not visible from this

transit location, so the transit has to be lowered or moved out from the centerline a bit, making a note of how far off the baseline it is.

Boarding the boat we measured the beam at a number of points to get the deckline in plan view. Then the overall length was measured. The forward and after overhangs were measured from the plumblines at each end.

The siding of the keel was measured at each station and the height from the bottom of the keel to the rabbet line taken. A detail sketch of the stem was made, with dimensions. The curve of the stem in profile was taken off with the transit set directly in front of the boat, using the same method as was used to take off stations. A big piece of cardboard was pressed against the transom, tracing around the transom to get its shape, then the centerboard slot in the bottom of the keel was located. The rudder and aft end of the keel were detailed. The mast, spars, and cabin details were measured to provide as much information as was desired to show on the drawings. If construction details are to be included, the scantlings and construction details are sketched and dimensioned. Often much of this detail is inaccessible.

With practice, the lines of a boat the size of *Pinkletink* can be taken off in five or six hours. In doing *Pinkletink* we used a homemade transit. This has the advantage of being much lighter to carry about than a genuine surveyor's transit, and is very, very much cheaper. You have to have use of a lathe, however, to make one, along with a bit of skill as a machinist.

Taking off lines when the boat is outdoors on blocks, or on a carriage or trailer is difficult, and not as accurate as it would be if the boat were on a good level floor. A floor makes a horizontal plane from which vertical measurements may be taken with accuracy.

On such a floor the transit is not necessary, and some mechanism for measuring vertical and horizontal distances is good. A simple diagram of such a device is shown in Figure 12. This will give a very accurate section — much better than it is possible to get with the "transit angle and distance" method used outdoors.

The data accumulated are worked up into a drawing by regular marine drafting methods, doing as little "fairing" as possible. Take more data than you think you will need. It is better to have too much than too little.

Chapter 5

THE BUILDING OF FRANCES
by Townsend Hornor

Being brought up in Osterville on the Cape is more or less synonymous with being brought up in catboats, or at least it used to be. For a very long time I thought that all boats with sails were gaff-rigged, and it was a pretty odd boat that did not have her mast up in her eyes. I had a series of little cat-rigged boats as a boy, including an incredible cat-rigged ketch all of 14 feet called the *Hymie Fink* that hardly tacked at all. My older brother, Jake, had a fat comfortable cat named *Katrina* of perhaps 24 feet with a live bait well in the cockpit where you could watch the bottom come up just as you ran aground. There were lots of cats, and lots of Crosbys, who ran the only two yards in Osterville, and still do. And then, starting with World War II, catboats began to fade. The gaff-rigged Wianno Senior knockabout, designed and built by H. Manley Crosby starting in about 1914 and still going strong (#151 and #152 were built during the winter of 1970-71, still of wood, thank goodness) held their own, but cats didn't. The tall marconi rig and the genoa jib and a serious wish for speed at the expense of comfort did a lot of the damage, and costs probably did the rest. As we all know, the passage of time in terms of catboats aging had nothing to do with it. Unlike people, catboats really do grow old gracefully, and imperceptibly.

Anyway, for whatever reasons, the last cat before *Frances* was built by Crosby Yacht Building and Storage Co. in 1935. And that seemed to me to be a very sad state of affairs. So, in about 1966 I started talking about building a cat with Bill Crosby, Jr.

Nobody, including Bill, took me very seriously for quite a while. Lots of people had brought up the same idea, but had invariably backed away when they learned how much stock it took to build a cat, and how much it might cost. But Bill and I had been pretty good friends for a long time, and he came to realize that I was serious and that I could stand shocks pretty well. Finally he became pretty enthusiastic, because it turned out that he really would like to build a cat, and that neither he nor any others of the younger generation at the yard had ever worked on a new one. The wheels were finally turning.

Fall of 1966 we found some fairly clear Virginia white cedar, bought a load of it, and set it aside to air-dry. (I noticed in reading up for this article that this seems to be a routine first step, whether you are building a cat or a Friendship — always white cedar.) We also started begging, scrounging, and stealing fittings such as boom bales, because we quickly discovered they weren't around much anymore. (Actually I think they are more readily available in 1972 with the great character-boat boom than they were in 1966.) On the way, we found in the back of a storeroom a beautiful tiller off a cat circa 1900, and decided to use it as we wanted a tiller anyway. We spent the winter settling on requirements and looking at catboat plans going back to 1885 or so. Most of these were in the Crosby files, but some were at Mystic and in old books. We finally decided that we wanted to build as small a cat as would take a minimum inboard engine, which seemed to mean something around

20 feet or a little more. We also wanted a smart sailer, and a pretty boat.

After a great deal of comparing and agonizing, we settled on a design by Wilton Crosby, Bill's great uncle, that he had built in 1900 for the Gurley family of Nantucket. The original boat had been named *Frances,* after an aunt of the owner, I believe. After many years Edouard Stackpole had acquired her, renamed her *Nantucket,* and brought her to Mystic when he was there as curator. In the spring of 1967, after securing a set of lines taken off her for Mystic by Ed Schock, we flew over to Nantucket on Easter Friday to see Mr. Stackpole. He was most gracious and helpful, showing us photographs and answering questions about her sailing qualities. While Bill and Brad Crosby and I talked with him, my wife Betsy and our two small children went for a long walk, and bought a Nantucket lightship basket in order to have a reason to stop somewhere to get warm. We added the cost to the catboat research account. At the end of the day we returned to Osterville convinced that we had the right basic hull design, and we also had Mr. Stackpole's kind permission to name her *Frances.* Following this trip, Bill Crosby, Sr., built a half model to the original lines, which further confirmed we were heading in the right direction.

During the summer of 1967, Bill developed a complete set of lines, deriving them from the original *Frances* plans, but making the small refinements that designers love to make. More importantly, he raised the sheer one strake, shortened the cabin trunk slightly, increased the cabin crown measurably from the typical flat one of the old boats, and modified the rig by modestly shortening the boom and lengthening the gaff as well as planning a somewhat higher peak. The net effect of all this was to reduce sail area somewhat. A curved bowsprit was added, to ease handling an anchor or mooring line. We have never regretted having the room to go forward of the mast, and it also improves her looks, in our opinion. After a lot of looking and debating, we decided to keep the overhanging stern and inboard rudder which, although difficult to build and therefore expensive, added greatly to her lines and were obviously functional when sailing at any angle of heel.

In the matter of an engine, our first thought was a make-and-break, which would seem to be appropriate to the boat, and they make such a nice sound early in the morning. Upon examination, it became apparent that it would have to have a reverse gear, as a concession to our children who would hopefully handle her in crowded harbors. Then we discovered that the overall length of an engine of this type plus reverse gear was too long for the space between the after end of the centerboard trunk and the inside of the deadwood. Finally, after looking at and discarding several currently available small engines, we found a 1956 Palmer Baby Husky 6 hp. This was rebuilt as new plus a starter-generator, and sold to us for the 1956 price with a new engine guarantee by Henry Zerbarini, a former Palmer master mechanic. It has proved totally satisfactory. For spars, we went to Pigeon, who turned out an elegant set in Sitka spruce, including a mast properly eight-sided from deck to step. Sailcloth was another concern — we didn't want a cotton sail, but neither did we like the dead white of modern synthetics. Bob Bainbridge came to our rescue with a dacron cloth dyed the color of Karnac, the longest staple Egyptian cotton. It's a lovely color, and easy on the eyes. Owen Torrey reached back to his Great South Bay catboat youth and cut the sail, very happily for us. Just to see Owen looking at a catboat sail after all his small boat, Olympic, and ocean racing experience was rewarding.

After the last boats were hauled and the Thanksgiving dishes cleared from the table in 1967, the building process really began, with Bill laying down the lines full size on the shop floor of the same boat shed where the original *Frances* had been built. Some good, straight Connecticut oak was selected for the keel, and a couple of natural crooks started to become the stem and stem knee. I learned the chore of cutting rabbets, a difficult task when you're not very good with adze or chisel. Later, I was allowed to drive the drifts for the centerboard and rudder, and I was better at that. About Christmas time the backbone was set up, ready to receive the centerboard box. The lower pieces of the box were 1½″ African mahogany, the upper, 1¼″ Honduras. They were tongue and grooved, and doweled to the keel. The standards were white oak. Next came the frames, steamed and then bent on a table in pairs, 1⅝″ square oak, fitted, dovetailed, and wedged into the keel. In proper catboat fashion, the frames forward of the centerboard box were closer, spaced on 10½″ centers, while those aft were on 12″ centers. We used four molds plus the transom onto which the ribbands were fastened, whereas in the old days they only used two, one at each end of the centerboard box, and the transom.

Frances *undergoing construction. (Robert R. Boulware)*

Floor timbers were white oak, as was the mast partner and the step, which was cross riveted for strength. Because of the somewhat tricky nature of the transom, a pine pattern was made first, followed by the final product in 1⅜″ western oak. Next came the planking, ⅞″ cedar, fastened with Everdur screws and with oak butt blocks. The original boat had cypress planking butted on the frames and iron nailed, which gives pause for thought when one considers how long she stayed in sailing shape — something like sixty years, admittedly with some help from time to time. Planking is a pretty interesting operation on a cat, particularly on a shapely one. Where the deadrise changes from the stem back into the forward bilges some special problems arise, calling for good stock and a first-class job. And aft, with her tumblehome and fairly extreme curves, it again has to be about right.

Decking is ⅝″ plywood on 1½″ x 2″ frames, spaced 10″, canvassed and painted. We had originally contemplated using a polypropylene and epoxy resin covering, but when we came down to it, it

44

Frances, *with Townie Hornor aboard, hits the water on launch day, April 13, 1968, at the Crosby Yacht Building and Storage Company yard, Osterville, Massachusetts. (Mystic Seaport)*

seemed inappropriate and we went back to the traditional material which past experience has shown to be good for thirty years if properly cared for. Similarly, the watertight self-bailing cockpit, also not on the original boat, was supposed to be poly over plywood, but we ended up with teak laid edge-grain because it looked so much better. The cabin trunk was interesting: along with increasing the camber to gain headroom, we also decided to eliminate the deck beams for the same reason. The top was built up out of three layers of 1/4″ plywood, glued on a form, installed and canvassed. The trunk sides and cockpit coaming are steam-bent mahogany, painted. Oak would have been used, but we could not seem to find any good bending stock. The cabin was ceiled up with Philippine mahogany, the vertical staving in the cockpit, Idaho pine, both with the same beading pattern as the original boat, although in her case the wood had been cypress. The rudder is western oak with Everdur drifts, with a bronze pipe stock and a bronze rudder port and stuffing box. The original boat had a wooden stock in a well, like a centerboard box. We increased the size of the rudder somewhat to compensate for the cutout of the deadwood for the propeller aperture. The centerboard

is of hard yellow pine, drifted, with an oak grounding shoe and about twenty pounds of lead.

The moldings, caps, door posts, hatch slide, toe rails, and whatever else in the trim department I may have forgotten are Honduras mahogany. Because of the width of the hatch slide, we beefed it up with a pair of teak stiffeners on its top, which also serve as handholds. The cabin was finished up rather simply, with a small head and two transom berths with the usual shelves under the deck. Inside ballast is 800 pounds of lead. Before launching we had to face the hardware problem in earnest. We wanted to use a pedestal or boom stool, to mount the boom gooseneck in the traditional way on the deck, rather than on the mast. Fortunately we found an old one in the shop and, using it as a pattern, Schaefer Marine made us one of stainless steel. We understand they are now making another one, which must make them the largest suppliers of boom stools in the Free World. For blocks we used Merriman wood-shell ash blocks. We found one boom bale in a rubbish pile under a workbench, and had two made using it as a pattern.

Then we came to the great gaff saddle experiment, wherein modern technology and materials once again lost out. Bill and I had been very impressed with the apparent success of the gaff saddle on the Marshall cats, and decided to adapt it to our purposes and eliminate that innate weakness of gaff rigs, the gaff jaws. It was a lovely idea, but it didn't work, perhaps because of our considerably heavier wooden gaff compared to the aluminum Marshall one. For whatever reason, the throat halyard and associated geometry became highly critical, and worsened as *Frances* came off the wind. Even liberal doses of tallow didn't help. After trying various modifications for two years, we discarded the new-fangled contraption and built a pair of oak jaws, laminated but otherwise in the traditional fashion with a goodly amount of turn, and the problem was solved. Running rigging is dacron, and the forestay 5/16″ 7x7 stainless, as is the bobstay. Finally she was ready for launching. Just for the record, her principal dimensions are 20′11″ loa, 18′6″ lwl, 9′5″ beam at decks, and 2′ draft with the board up.

Saturday, April 13, 1968, dawned clear and bright as they say, which was to be expected inasmuch as it was Passover, the day before Easter, at the height of a full moon, and launching day. No sense in doing things on inauspicious days, if auspicious ones are just as convenient. A goodly crowd gath-

Frances spanks along on a close reach. Wilton B. (Bill) Crosby, Jr., her builder, is on the sheet; Townie Hornor, her owner, is at the helm, 1969. (Norman Fortier)

ered, including our friends from Nantucket, Mr. Stackpole, Pinkie and John Leavens from Chilmark, and others. Our daughter Grace, then of ten tender years, was the sponsor. Unfortunately for her, the champagne bottle had apparently been built by the French branch of the Crosby family, and was just as tough as *Frances'* stem, resulting in a tie. Finally Mother, a veteran of many launchings, helped out, spilling a modest amount of her blood in the process, and *Frances* was duly christened. Her proud owner rode her into the water, hand firmly on tiller, and could not be persuaded to let go for the rest of the day, even for food or drink.

The week after saw the mast stepped, the running rigging reeved and a proper "glut" (an Oscar Pease term of art) installed under the deck on the after side of the mast to prevent the possibility of the mast lifting out of the step in a heavy seaway. The sail was seized on the hoops, slides installed on the tracks, outhauls made up, and we were sailing. She proved up to her promise, showing herself to be a smart sailer, easy to tack even with the board up, and satisfactory in every way. She is a complete credit to her designers and builders, as an able and handsome wooden cat.

Chapter 6

FIBERGLASS CATBOATS
by Breck Marshall

The use of fiberglass has brought new life to the classic American catboat. Breck Marshall, who pioneered in the use of fiberglass for cats in 1962-1963, gives the ins and outs of this new material. His successful 18-foot Sanderling and 22-foot model recently joined by a new 15'6" half-decked cat, Sandpiper, have prompted a number of imitators, among them:

- *The Chappiquidick Twenty Five built in Taiwan (also built in wood).*
- *The 17½-foot Wittholz-Hermann cabin cat called the Cape Cod Cat.*
- *The Americat 22 modeled after a Sweisguth design of the 1920's.*
- *The 18½-foot Herreshoff America designed by Halsey Herreshoff.*

Many small fiberglass cats have also recently come into production, including Merv Hammatt's 14-foot cuddy cat, Cape Dory's 14-foot Handy Cat to Merle Hallet's design, Osterville Marine's 14-foot Crosby Fast Cat, and the 16-foot Sun Cat.

John M. Leavens

Fiberglass catboats are gaining rapidly in numbers since I built the first production fiberglass catboat in 1962/63. At present there are several different makers of fiberglass catboats other than those made by the Marshall Company. Among them is the Wittholz-Hermann cat, a 17½-footer formerly made on Long Island and now made by Cape Cod Shipbuilding Company, and the Americat 22 made by George Benedict's Vintage Boat Company at Sayville on Long Island.

The Marshall Company builds three catboats, the 18-foot Sanderling, named for the small shorebird familiar along the New England seashore, a 22-footer that as yet has no name, and the new 15'6" Sandpiper.

The 18-foot Sanderling was first built in 1961/62 at New Boston, New Hampshire when I was work-ing for Gilbert Verney. The prototype was a wood catboat designed by Pop Arnold in 1941. When Verney and I set out to build the first fiberglass catboat, we chose Pop Arnold's basic design because I had inherited the plans and three or four of the station molds from my days of service working for Bill Tripp at East Greenwich, Rhode Island.

The original was not a pretty boat. She had a flat sheer with a kind of tumblehome ram bow in her. She had a square house on her and a marconi rig. My foreman and I spent about three weeks in the visual process of modeling by eye. First we took the Number 1 station and hollowed it out quite a bit. We pulled the stem out a bit and gave it a little overhang. We couldn't give her the tumblehome bow of the original or we wouldn't get her out of the molds very well. In setting each suc-

The Marshall 22, *which was first built in 1965. She is 22'2" overall, 10'2" beam, 2' draft with the board up, and 5'5" draft with the board down. She carries 404 square feet of sail.*

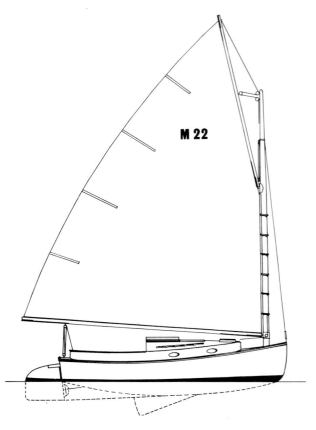

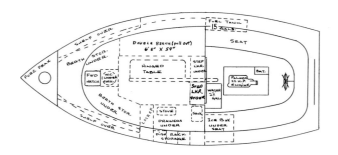

The 18' 2" Marshall Sanderling, first of the production-line fiberglass cats, set the stage in 1963 for the emergence of the catboat as a class racer.

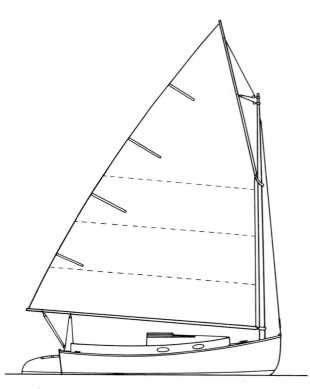

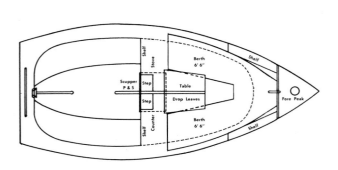

ceeding station, we gave her more sheer than the original boat had. We spent a long time modeling the boat, but both when we started and when we were through, we had no lines anywhere that pictured the boat.

We built a couple of Sanderlings and got one ready just in time for the boat show in February, 1963. We had quite a reception. We were "the boat from New Hampshire" all by ourselves. People that saw it were charmed, but they just couldn't imagine a catboat built in New Hampshire. I heard one fisherman say to his crony, "some crackpot in New Hampshire is building this."

Well, it *was* crazy to build them in the backwoods of New Hampshire. We built eleven boats that year and only sold four of them, plus one hull that went to Macy Webster. About November of 1963, Gil Verney wanted to give up, so I bought the catboat operation and the boats left over. I paid him a fairly good price, and all of a sudden I had the Marshall Company. I was the only one in it.

As a first step, the boats and gear were brought down to salt water, the natural habitat of the catboat, at Padanarum — the town of South Dartmouth where we are now located. There were boats in garages and breezeways and out in the fields. Yet, that winter, all were sold, chiefly because we had changed the address to Massachusetts. It's a funny thing. People don't think you can build a boat in the backwoods. After the move, we kept on getting orders, and every winter demand has increased. We had confidence enough by 1965 to go ahead with the bigger cat — the 22-footer. The first one was *Grimalkin* in 1965.

The 18-footer is 2,200 pounds with everything aboard and in the water, but without stores or engine. The 22-footer is about 5,650 pounds. She's more refined and sharper in the bow. The assumption is that the smaller the boat, the more hollow the bow should be. The small boat can't just bust her way through seas. A wave is a pretty massive thing, and you can't go at it in a small boat as you would in a 75-footer. In the Marshall fiberglass boats, there is no deadwood at all from the stem right back to the center of the centerboard trunk. That's half of the boat. The old-time cats had to have deadwood or an outside keel the full length to fasten the garboards to. In a fiberglass boat, all that beefing up is inside the boat, so they are quite fair forward.

In light airs, the 18-footer generally beats the

Sandpiper. This smart 15' 6" open-cockpit daysailer is the newest addition (1972) to the family of Marshall fiberglass cats. (The Marshall Company, Norman Fortier)

bigger one. She has no propeller to drag, for one thing. At, say, ten knots of wind the advantage that the 18-footer has over the 22-footer disappears. The 22-footer has three times the displacement and a lot more pounds per square foot of sail area. It also has propeller drag, which is quite considerable in light airs, but if you get anything beyond six knots the propeller drag is less important.

That's how we got the fiberglass catboat started, how we brought her from New Hampshire down to salt water where she's supposed to be, and so got her established. Business is booming now and we have a hard time keeping up with orders. Fiberglass is the reason the business is booming.

Fiberglass is an ideal material for boat-building because it is flexible and strong for its unit weight. With fiberglass, all sorts of curves can be reproduced. In fact, compound curvature in fiberglass gives greater strength than in other materials. The way we build our catboats, the only joint line is where the deck and hull meet, and this is strongly

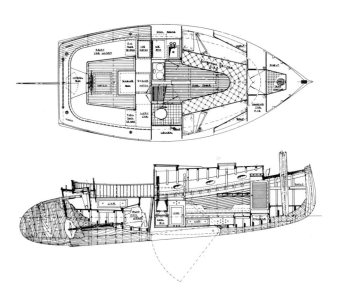

The Chappiquiddick Twenty Five designed by Edward S. Brewer and built, beginning in 1970, in Taiwan in wood or fiberglass for One Design Marine, Inc.

bonded. The result is a monocoque, the two parts — deck and hull — becoming one single unit. In contrast, a wood boat, by its nature, with thousands of fastenings, has to work. As a consequence, the wood boat isn't as stiff as a fiberglass boat.

A fiberglass hull, given the molds and plugs, can be turned out in a fraction of the time that it takes to build a wood boat. Although a set of molds will cost six or seven times what it would cost to build a wood boat, the molds can be used over and over again, up to 100 times, to produce fiberglass boats at a considerable overall saving in unit costs. We are up to hull number 202 in the Sanderling model and are on our third set of molds. We reproduce each new set of molds from an existing hull in order to maintain the integrity of the lines.

Fiberglass is durable and requires considerably less maintenance than a wood boat. So the saving in upkeep is in addition to the saving in original cost.

To make a fiberglass boat one must first make a complete wooden boat hull. We build the wood hull upside down because it is to serve as the parent for the female mold and it is easier to see the imperfections. This hull need not be structurally

strong, but the shape must be perfect and the hull has to be absolutely smooth and fair. In a wooden boat you can get away with a seam that shows or with a little dig here or there in the surface, but the parent of the fiberglass boat must be absolutely perfect or the imperfections will show up on each finished fiberglass boat.

We spend hours and hours filling imperfections in the wood prototype hull with body putty and then sanding them smooth. We use belt sanders sometimes, but we find it better to use strips of wood about three feet long and six inches wide and attach the paper to that. With these strips, we go back and forth across the grain of the wood and take off the high spots. Then we spray the hull with a lacquer finish and get a real sheen. When the hull is perfectly smooth and fair, we apply three or four coats of wax before we lay the fiberglass over it.

In building the female mold, we take the same steps as if we were going to build a fiberglass boat. We use rolls of fiberglass mat and lay it over the hull. That captures the exact shape. Like a dentist taking an impression of a tooth, we get an exact reproduction of the original. When we are finished,

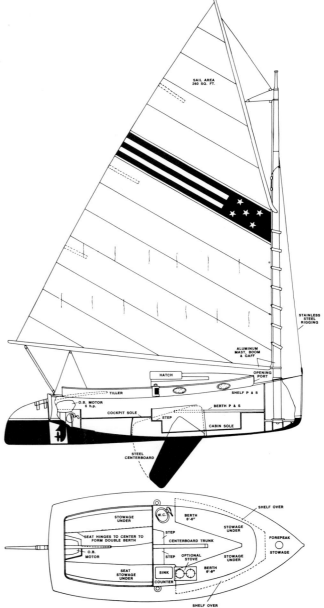

The Handy Cat is a 14-foot Cape Cod open-cockpit catboat designed by Merle Hallet in 1970 and built by Cape Dory Co., Inc.

Halsey Herreshoff designed the Nowak and Williams 18' 2" Herreshoff America fiberglass catboat in 1971.

we pull the whole female mold off the plug, turn it right side up, and we are ready to build boats.

In building a fiberglass boat, we use the hand lay-up method as distinct from the spraying method which, however, is an effective way of doing small parts. In the hand lay-up method, alternate layers of mat and roving are applied to the female mold. In mat, the crossed fibers go in all directions. Roving is a very coarse burlap. Both bond well with fiberglass resin. Fiberglass cloth is woven with parallel fibers. The cloth looks nice, but it doesn't bond with the resin as well as mat and roving to produce the strength we want, so we don't use it. The rolls of fiberglass mat and roving are factory produced and are of constant density. Every time a whole ply is laid down against the female mold, an exact and known quantity of material is placed in position. Each ply is saturated with resin and smoothed out to the proper shape. Each ply takes a little less than an hour to cure.

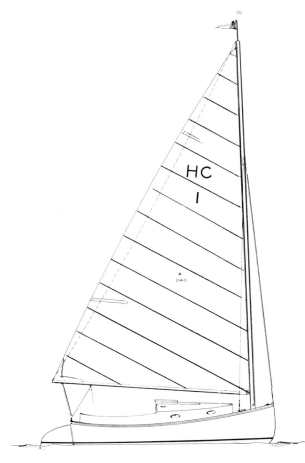

Charles W. Wittholz-designed, 17-foot fiberglass Hermann catboat, first built in 1967, comes in optional marconi or gaff rig.

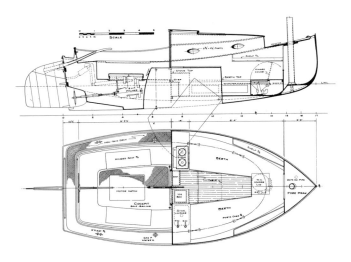

In building our 22-footer, we use seven basic plies with beefed-up areas in the garboard down in the bilge where it turns up in the centerboard trunk. There we put an additional four plies for a total of eleven, carrying them up to strengthen the centerboard trunk. Similarly, we put down eleven plies in the forepeak area where the mast step is located. The step itself is built out of 25 plies in a special step mold and is set in its place in the bow with secondary fiberglass bonds that are extremely strong.

Where the hull and deck meet, we use a special bonding process. No mechanical fasteners are employed. The hull and deck are joined together at a tangent. Inside of that joint we use successive bonding strips of fiberglass. First a four-inch strip goes all across the crack where the hull and deck meet. Then we apply successively a six-inch strip, an eight-inch strip, and a 10-inch strip, each of which goes futher inboard and down on the hull. In effect, a heavy fillet is formed where the hull and deck join. This is a secondary bond and it is extremely strong.

The centerboard trunk is integral with the hull. A male plug is pushed up through the hole in the bottom of the hull. This is heavily waxed, and the plies are then built on this plug, the secondary bond going down over the garboards and up over the hull. When all is finished, the male plug is removed and the centerboard, separately built out of fiberglass, is fitted in place.

The final finish is a gel coat. This surface coat, similar to a heavy paint coat, is basically a resin with heavy pigments in it. It is much more viscous than resin and it can be colored. Ned Lund's Sanderling *Red Squirrel* is actually red, the color being pigment added to the gel coat.

The rudder, hatches, and cabin slides are built separately of fiberglass. The rudder is about one-sixth the length of the boat. For example, the 18-footer has a three-foot rudder. Also, I leave the rudder square on the lower end in order to get more bite.

All our spars are aluminum extrusions. The mast is a standard elliptical extrusion with a taper in the top. The taper is seven and a half feet in the 18-

footer and nine feet in the 22-footer. This taper is achieved by spinning the extrusion in a lathe and squeezing the tubing at the same time. The result is that the wall thickness of the tube at the top is greater than it is at the bottom. It is esthetically pleasing, but it also provides the greatest strength in the working part of the mast. We fill the bottom six feet of the mast with a dense foam for structural reasons. This strengthens the mast against the risk of breaking just above the deck. Engineers say that it would take 920 pounds at the tip of the mast to break it, but by that time the boat would have tipped over.

The boom and gaff are standard extrusions but without any taper. In attaching the gaff to the mast, we use a saddle because we couldn't come up with any way to fit wooden jaws to an aluminum gaff, and metal jaws would chafe too much. We developed a saddle to suit our needs, and we line it with vinyl held in place by flush rivets so that it won't score the mast. The saddle is held to the mast by a line of parrels.

We have built 202 of the 18-foot Sanderlings and 45 of the 22-footers. All are heavily built of fiberglass with more plies than any other comparable stock boats. The steady market for new Marshall cats is a good index of the value of fiberglass as a new material for boatbuilding. However, perhaps a better sign of the worth of fiberglass is the heavy demand for second-hand Marshall cats in the used boat market. Someone always seems to be looking for one of them.

Chapter 7

A FERRO-CEMENT CAT
by Trent H. Holmes

Ferro-cement has also emerged in the last few years as a new material for catboats. A 17-foot keel ferro-cement cat has recently been built on the West Coast to a design by Jay R. Benford of Seattle, Washington. Trent Holmes, of Rocky Hill, Con- *necticut, designed and built, with the help of Dr. Hans F. Waecker, the mammoth 34-foot catboat Meow using the English Seacrete process. In this chapter, he describes this new ferro-cement material.*

John M. Leavens

In the Spring of 1967, I was planning a trip to England and, as chance would have it, I read an article in the British magazine *Light Steam Power* concerning a process of constructing boats from concrete. Such boats were being made in England by Windboats, Ltd., in Wroxham, Norfolk. The product is called Seacrete. According to the article, Windboats had been building boats of Seacrete for about eight years. It sounded quite interesting, but I will admit I was skeptical, and had many questions.

Subsequently, I took my trip and, of course, made a visit to Wroxham. Windboats is a very neat and tidy operation owned by Donald Hagenbach, President. Donald showed me around the boatyard and we shook and pounded a 34-foot hull which had survived an explosion and fire. The hull was basically sound and solid. My interest in Seacrete increased by leaps and bounds.

We started discussing the possibility of a catboat hull of this, to me, new material. Many hours were spent going over methods and sketches with Donald and his staff, to see just how Seacrete could best be used to create a catboat. I was sold on Seacrete,

but in spite of the many hours that we spent going over details, specifications, and Seacrete design requirements, I left England with many unanswered questions and faced a complete redesign with a whole new rule book.

Many of the structural requirements and space-consuming methods used for wood construction no longer applied. In place of frames 3 inches thick plus 1½ inches of planking, I now had a total skin thickness of ⅞ inch. The solid oak keel/skeg was replaced by a hollowed-out area. Engines could be relocated deep and in the fore-and-aft center where weight helped. Drive gear became conventional. Joints between skin and wells did not exist. Now we could use centerboards; yes, two, one forward to help offset the weather helm, and one conventionally aft.

New designs, new lines, new arrangements all had to be started, so I could get prints to England for comments and quotations. Many letters flew between the USA and Wroxham. Questions on methods of attaching the deck, suitable engines, tanks, fittings, material sizes, and spacing of floors had to be resolved. Now I needed answers to many

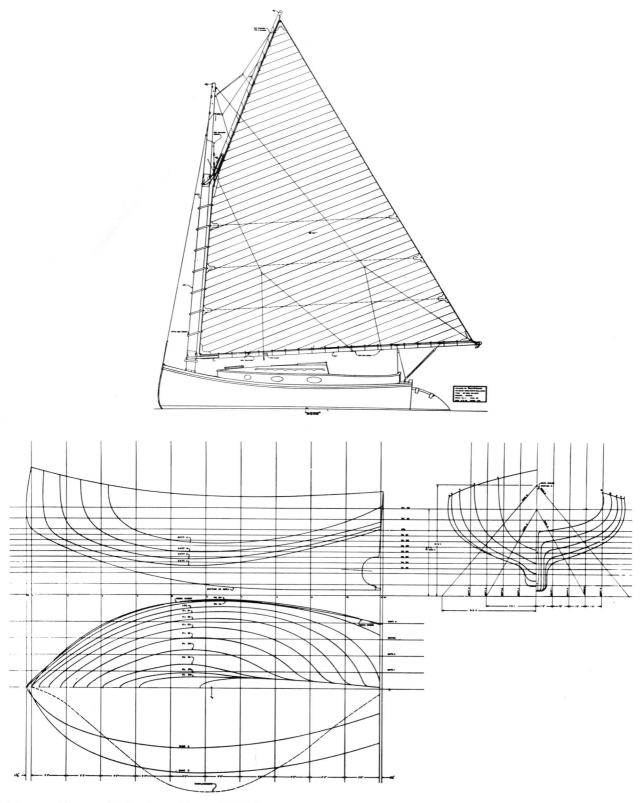

Meow — *lines and sail plan. (Trent H. Holmes)*

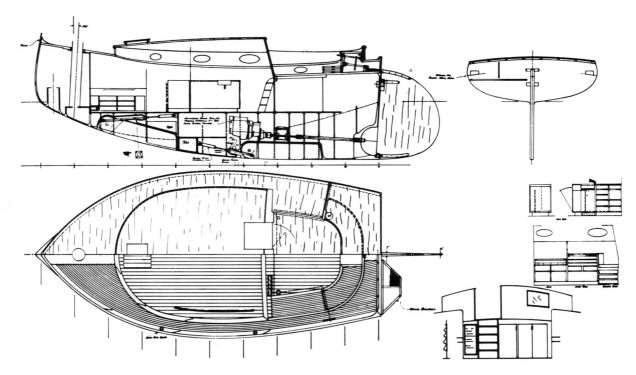

Meow — inboard profile and deck plan. (Trent H. Holmes)

questions which presented themselves as I was working out the detailed plans. Frequently I found that the experience of Windboats, Ltd., did not cover what I wanted to design. Time was passing and Windboats was getting busy with orders for many other boats. My problems were not being solved for several months at a time. Then I received a letter from Donald, telling me that he was going to be visiting Canada and the States on business. He said he would have a hull in the Boston Boat Show. I sent a list of questions for him to answer so that we could go over them first-hand while he visited me.

My wife, Jean, had not seen a Seacrete hull, so we took a trip to the Boston Show to see the display, meet Donald, and also meet Dr. Hans Waecker, the owner of the display hull and prospective licensee of Seacrete in this country. Marinecrete of Portland, Maine, resulted from this visit. A contract for our catboat hull was soon signed with Dr. Waecker. Now Hans's problems were just starting. He went to England to gain first-hand experience on ferro-cement construction procedures as practiced by Windboats, Ltd. Upon returning to Portland, he started assembling equipment in a rented area of the Story Marine Railway (the yard

has since been sold and is now called South Portland Shipyard). He hired people to man the equipment and to be trained in the techniques of ferro-cement boat construction.

Meow was designed and tested in model form before construction began. As construction lofting progressed, a complete set of detailed structural drawings was made in which ferro-cement methods and my accommodation requirements were combined to try and get the best combination of both. The general method of construction was to set up frames of solid rod or pipe. I prefer solid ½-inch diameter rod because it bends easily and produces less bulk and hull thickness. Onto these rods were fastened ¼-inch diameter stringers on 2-inch centers. Added to these were two more layers of ½-inch mesh uncoated hardware cloth. The whole assembly is held together with wire ties and pounded into a fair shape. The final operation of pounding into shape is most critical and requires a lot of time and a good eye to make sure there are no high spots or hollows. The whole framework was then plastered by hand trowel from both inside and out with a Portland cement and sand mix. After the initial set, the structure was allowed to cure under a fine water spray for two weeks.

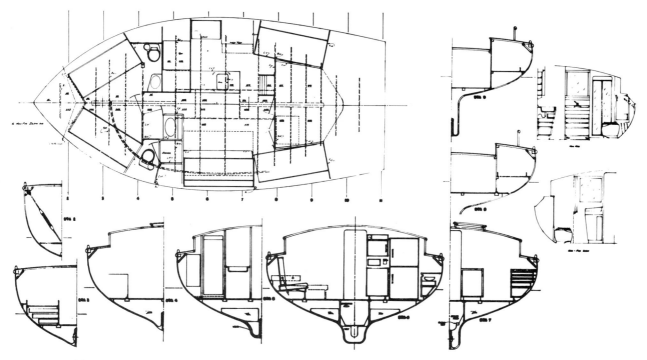

Meow — *cabin layout. (Trent H. Holmes)*

This technique has produced an exceptionally strong hull, as was borne out by two incidents since launching. While we were still in Portland, Maine, we were moved to a four-foot diameter spherical mooring float made of 3/16-inch welded steel. On one weekend while we were aboard in a flat calm, the float kept nudging the hull with a rather loud resounding drum sound. A yacht passed by with gay sightseers to take a closer look, and they kicked up quite a wake, so that the float and *Meow* came together with a terrible crash. From the sound, I thought sure that damage had been done. I ran to the bow and looked over, but could not see any damage. I got in the dinghy for a closer inspection: there was no hull damage, but quite a bit of paint from the float was on the unpainted hull. The float told another story. There were nine depressions ranging in size from three to five inches, all fresh, with abrasion marks from the concrete, indicating that it and *Meow* had been making violent contact in the past, probably the result of other speedy sightseers.

The second incident occurred when we were at a dock for service. A 30-footer had its rudder jam while maneuvering and caught *Meow's* stern corner about midship on his beam. We lost a corner

about two inches high and half inch deep of unreinforced concrete. We took off about two feet of his rub rail, gouged his toe rail, and cracked his plywood deck. A little epoxy putty on our stern corner made it as good as new.

I might mention here that when designing a boat to be made of ferro-cement, all details should be thoroughly thought out and accurately specified on the design. Additions and changes are very difficult to make after the hull is finished. Even with the background gained in England, and the help from on-the-job English personnel, many problems had to be worked out during construction.

The metal lay-up, for example, required a hardware cloth wire mesh, which was not available in this country. It was ordered from England. Progress was being made, until an East Coast dock strike held up delivery of the mesh. Local material was tried as a substitute, but it was found not to be ductile enough, and therefore would not conform to the hull contour without a lot of added work.

One problem of interest was posed by a requirement that I did not want any iron exposed to sea water or outside of the cement shell. Marinecrete felt that a steel plate was needed along the keel to support the balance of the steel work. The prob-

The massiveness of Meow, *a 32-foot catboat designed by Trent H. Holmes and built of Seacrete, shows up as she is hauled out in 1971 at Portland, Connecticut. (Alfred R. Sears)*

lem was how to support this steel keel and yet get concrete on the lower or outer surface. A steel framework was made with projecting adjustable studs. These studs were threaded into the bottom of the keel plate with space between the keel and frame to allow for wire mesh and the plastering operation. Problems of this type presented quite a challenge to construction.

When the hull was completed and cured, the engines were installed and the exterior joiner work was undertaken at Portland by master carpenter George D. Smith. The materials used for this construction were oak, teak, and marine-grade fir plywood. The deck is teak over pre-formed plywood, made up of four layers of ¼-inch material, formed over a temporary frame and epoxy-glued to each other. The deck is bolted to an oak clamp, which in turn is bolted through the ferro-cement. The oak rub rail is also bolted through the hull and clamp. The teak toe rail is bolted through the deck and clamp.

The cabin sole is made of plywood sheets, with areas between two and ten square feet. The sole is supported on a gridwork of oak, which in turn is bolted to the ferro-cement floors. This enables any one section of the sole to be lifted without disturbing the others.

The rudder is oak, bolted with bronze. Steering is with a modified Edson quadrant gear. The centerboards are oak, bolted with bronze, and slide-in sheet-bronze liners are in the ferro-cement wells. Actuation of the centerboards is with hydraulic cylinders, operating through flexible sea-water gland seals.

While the exterior joiner work was being done in Maine, I was busy at home in Connecticut making tanks, a variable-pitch propeller, chart table, galley unit, etc., all of which we took to Maine and installed in *Meow*. I also made provision for a davit hole to be fabricated in the engine well area so that a collapsible davit could be installed for removing the engines.

The deck and cabin work progressed, but at a very slow pace. At times it seemed we would never get *Meow* to Connecticut. Finally, the day for launching arrived, June 12, 1971. We were to be in Maine about noon, and the launch would be in the early afternoon, at high tide. When we arrived, complete with checklist of things to do before the launch, we were surprised to see *Meow* sitting out at the end of the railway in her cradle with the water lapping at her keel. *Meow* had been inadvertently launched. It seems that the people of the boatyard wanted to make everything ready for a smooth launch, by greasing the wheels on the flat car, then easing it down on the inclined part of the track. But the winch was unwinding cable faster than the boat was moving, and a few turns of cable unwound from the drum and became fouled in the machinery. About this time the boat started moving, came to the end of the fouled cable, which promptly broke, allowing the boat, cradle, and flat car to continue on past the end of the track. All efforts to return the boat were in vain, so as the eleven-foot tides came in, *Meow* was water-borne and leaking.

We had to get aboard quickly, and connect the batteries (one of the items on my before-launch checklist) so the automatic bilge pump would start doing its job. By the time we got aboard and connected the batteries, the water was just touching the bottom of the engine crankcase. We estimated about 500 gallons had come in, based on the time

Looking aft at the interior layout of Benford's 17-foot ferrocement cat. (Roy Montgomery)

it took two 1,300-gallon-per-hour pumps to bring the level down to a few inches.

We were heartsick. The boat was committed, sink or float, and we had no way to rehaul because the railway was still out of commission. After the initial gallonage was pumped out, one pump was just able to keep it under control running five out of every six minutes. We put the batteries on sustaining shore charge, removed the propulsion engine and generator, plugged as many of the dozens of pinholes with beeswax, wooden plugs, and underwater epoxy as best we could from the inside. As we plugged the lower areas, new areas would start seeping further up. We stayed aboard two anxious nights.

When we left at the end of that long weekend, the pump was still running five minutes out of six. The next weekend we drove the 200 miles back to Maine not knowing what to expect. Much to our surprise, the pump was running at a slower cycle, about four minutes out of six. Original areas which were leaking had subsided, and new pinhole areas had appeared. There was some rust coming through and it appeared that the iron of the mesh was oxidizing. Our confidence was bolstered to the point that we took *Meow* out for trials in the harbor. The propulsion and generator engines both ran, and all seemed well. So we started to lay plans for our trip home.

By the time we were ready for the run home, the leaks had reduced to the point where the pump was running one minute out of fifteen, and each day on the trip home we noticed a reduction in pump running time until the end of the trip it was running one minute in several hours. After the first efforts to stem the flow, I did nothing more, so all

Jay R. Benford of Seattle, Washington, designed this 17-foot ferrocement cat in 1972. (Roy Montgomery)

the subsequent reduction was brought about by the self-healing action of iron oxide. I have reason to believe that a major crack caused by the collision would heal in the same way, provided a pump of adequate size were available to take on the first onslaught of water inflow.

On the trip down, off Boston Light and into the Cape Cod Canal, we had the tail of the hurricane Beth building up short eight-foot rollers. These were coming in under our port stern quarter. *Meow* didn't seem to mind a bit. She sat like a gull, and didn't take a drop of water over the side. I might note that *Meow* did not have a mast, and the whole trip was under power. We also did not have any ballast, and were running about eight tons less than the designed nineteen long tons displacement. The stern was just about on designed waterline, but the bow was riding about two feet high. This would be corrected with tanks, ballast, mast, anchor chain, furnishings, etc.

The last leg of our journey home was up the Connecticut River, and the only time we took water over the bow was in the river when a large cruiser sent a wake which we caught just right, so that it sent a sheet of water about ten feet into the air.

Now the boat is hauled in Portland, Connecticut, so that I may finish the interior. The hull is unpainted, mainly because I have not found a paint for ferro-cement which I consider reliable. We picked up quite a bit of marine growth, and a few barnacles, which dried up and could be brushed off after we hauled. During this cleaning process, my wife asked, "What is this hole?" I looked, and found it was a ⅝-inch hole used to support the original steel shoe in the first part of the framing construction. The stud had been removed and the hole was left and never plugged. That was the source of our leak, and it was never filled or detected because it was right at a spot where the hull rested on the original construction launching cradle. The hole is now plugged and other work proceeds.

A few comments on the characteristics of Seacrete as a material for boats can be made:

- Hull noise seems to be a little greater than wood, but quite a bit less than fiberglass or metal.
- Vibration from the two rubber-mounted diesel engines is almost undetectable, and engine noise is not transmitted through the hull.
- The hull will sweat below the waterline during long rain periods or damp weather. This is due to the cold water outside chilling the hull and condensing moisture from the air. An insulating coating will overcome this problem.
- Material can be readily bonded to the hull with epoxy, polyester, or polyurethane, all of which adhere well and appear to offer a permanent bond under water.
- Even though the hull has over two tons of steel in it, there does not appear to be any strong adverse affect on the compass. Compensation was readily provided with the built-in adjusting screws.

We look forward to the time when the final details of the interior work are finished, our mast is stepped, our sail is bent, and *Meow* becomes the full-fledged cat that she was designed to be. The promise at this stage of her development is most encouraging.

Chapter 8

THE BEETLE CAT
by Waldo Howland

Catboats come in all sizes from 12 feet to 48 feet. The cats at the small end of the range are never cabin boats and rarely open boats. More often they are half-decked craft with large open cockpits and decked-over forepeaks. Occasionally they have a small cuddy or shelter cabin. In every respect, however, they are true cats. Some are unique productions such as Marionette *built at Mattapoisett, Massachusetts, in 1888 by Alonzo Jenny and recently bought by 13-year-old Bob Stuart of Cohasset, Massachusetts. Edson Schock of Kingston, Rhode Island, designed and built a fast able daysailer cat for his own use.* Trio, *on exhibit at Mystic Seaport, was one of several similar cats built by the Crosbys of Osterville around the turn of the century. Charles Anderson, a well-known catboat builder of* Wareham, Massachusetts, *turned out a fleet of fifty decked 15-foot cats around 1900. Now and then one of them comes to light.*

There continues to be a lively interest in the small daysailer cat, as is evidenced by the five new fiberglass cats referred to in the introduction to Chapter 6.

The most popular and best known small cat is the 12'4" Beetle Cat first built in 1921 by members of the same family that produced the famous Beetle whaleboat. In 1946 the Concordia Company, Inc., of South Dartmouth, Massachusetts, took over production of the Beetle Cat. Waldo Howland, who until a year or so ago headed the Concordia Company, writes about the Beetle.

John M. Leavens

I'm quite sure that there are not many classes of sailboats that have celebrated a 50th anniversary. In fact, I do not know of any widely used class boat other than the Beetle Cat that was designed and built fifty years ago, and still continues to be built unchanged and sailed today. Some folks quite reasonably ask, why retain the old design and construction when new shapes and methods are being developed? I can only say that the virtues and challenges of the winds and the waves have not changed, and a pleasure boat design that was good fifty years ago is still good today. In reading an English manual, republished in 1880, I came across an article on "Una" boats. Una means "one", I am told, and in this case refers to a boat with one sail; it also refers to a boat of the same name that made the type popular in England. The design illustrated was some 16' long and was originally built in Bayonne, New Jersey. She looks almost exactly like a Beetle Cat, in both hull shape and rig. The article states that "these wonderful little craft" were "extremely handy and useful, and would always be popular."

We all know that no boat can do everything, or suit everyone's needs. In fact, an old fellow told me "that any boat built for everyone is, in fact, built for no one." Originally, sailing craft were used mainly for cargo, fishing, or fighting. Only in more recent years have they been developed for pleasure. Fifty years ago and more, many folks and their families took their boating pleasure in day sailing, in fishing, in beach picnics, and the like. For these purposes a small catboat was, and is, ideally suited. These boats are displacement hulls, are stable, roomy, handy, shoal draft, can be beached, and are seaworthy for harbor and bay sailing.

The Beetle Cat rig is similar to that used on old large-size Cape Cod catboats, with the mast well forward and using a single gaff-rigged sail. With this type of rig, if you release the tiller the boat will head into the wind and practically stop. This feature makes it an ideal boat for youngsters. You can shorten sail with a gaff-rigged catboat and still keep the center of the sail effort where you want it without fear of the boat taking charge and falling off. All sheets and halyards are handled from the cockpit. No backstays to tend. No headsails to trim.

The bow of the Beetle Cat is generous in proportion, so that even an extra-large man can stand on it without tipping over — a feature that is much appreciated when landing at a dock or float. The fact that the mast is short and the deck is long reduces to a minimum the possibility that such a boat may capsize while riding at its moorings, even in exposed locations where seas become decidedly heavy. Just step aboard this little boat and you get the feel of a boat twice her size with its comfortable cockpit.

Currently there is great enthusiasm for racing, almost to the exclusion of just sailing for the pure fun of it. I, too, have enjoyed racing. Starting in the 1930's, I had the fun and excitement of racing International 14-footers in England during a Cowes Week Regatta. Later I raced in light displacement types known as B Dinghies, which were especially active in frostbite regattas. These were all light-displacement planing hulls similar, in most ways, to the many modern planing hulls. I kept a B Dinghy at Padanaram for several years, but there was no racing class of such boats here at that time, and I learned that for family day sailing, fishing, beaching, etc., she had real limitations. What I am attempting to say is that sailboats of all kinds can be fun and useful, but each individual should try to figure out how he or she will be using his boat: what the conditions will be like in his area, where he will moor or dock his boat, etc. Only after deciding on these things, and remembering how old, or how young you are, can you best choose a boat for your own use.

Just as the design of hull chosen should be a matter of individual taste and requirements, rather than a current trend, or style, so too is the construction of a boat a feature for each prospective sailor to consider carefully. The newer materials, such as fiberglass, aluminum, etc., all have their real merits and enthusiastic promoters and followers. One has only to pick up any current boating magazine, or observe any local fleet, to be convinced of this. For some people, however, there are, or can be, basic virtues in wood construction that materially enhance their pleasure in owning a boat. Wood has been used successfully in boatbuilding for centuries. The cedars of Lebanon are mentioned in the Bible for boatbuilding, and wood has always been the most suitable material for many applications. Beetle Cat boats are built of wood, as is my father's desk, and my own dining room table, and the maestro's fiddle. There is something pleasing about the appearance and the feel which is probably mostly aesthetic. However, native cedar sprung over steam-bent white oak frames does produce a very fair hull, one that is strong and quiet, and intrinsically buoyant. The original cost of a Beetle is not high when compared with other finished boats of the same general size. Given intelligent care, the life of a Beetle has been, in many cases, forty years or more. If faced honestly, I feel that any piece of equipment, boat or other, must be given some care and maintenance, or else be of the disposable type. Wood definitely does require special attention, but annual maintenance can be a pleasure or a problem, just depending on one's situation, point of view, and how one goes about it. Maintenance of a boat has often been pictured as a terrible devouring monster, but there are people who like to work in the garden, build model cars, or work on their boat. If one enjoys working with his hands and has the good fortune to have the time, then his efforts on a wood boat can be very rewarding and be a continuing pleasure during the winter months.

In addition to the basic good qualities of a small wooden catboat, the Beetles have developed into a racing class of long standing and popularity. There are now over three thousand Beetles in existence, and over thirty active racing fleets. There is a wonderful and dedicated Beetle Cat Boat Association that guides and promotes Beetle racing rules and activities. Three or four times each winter the Board of Governors gathers in New Bedford from different parts of New England to consider and act

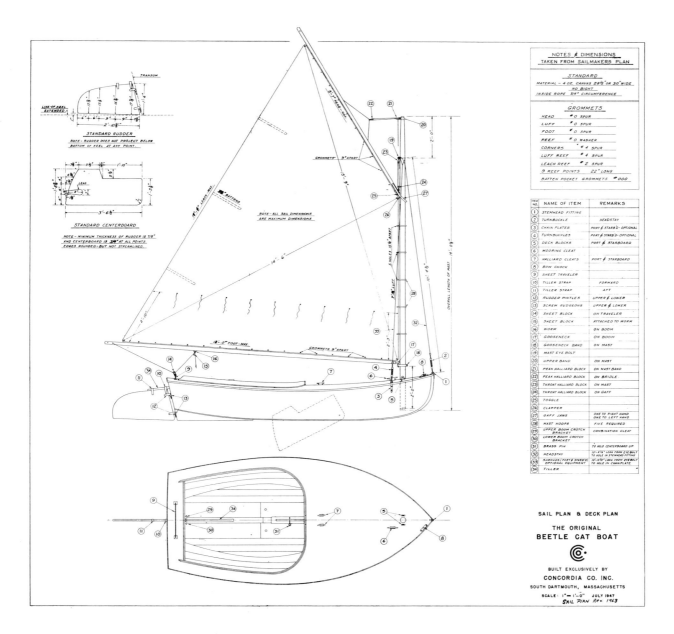

NOTES & DIMENSIONS
TAKEN FROM SAILMAKERS PLAN

STANDARD
MATERIAL - 4 OZ. CANVAS 28½" OR 30" WIDE
NO BIGHT
INSIDE ROPE 3/4" CIRCUMFERENCE

GROMMETS

HEAD	# O SPUR	
LUFF	# O SPUR	
FOOT	# O SPUR	
REEF	# O WASHER	
CORNERS	# 4 SPUR	
LUFF REEF	# 4 SPUR	
LEACH REEF	# 2 SPUR	
9 REEF POINTS	22" LONG	
BATTEN POCKET GROMMETS	# 000	

ITEM NO.	NAME OF ITEM	REMARKS
1	STEMHEAD FITTING	
2	TURNBUCKLE	HEADSTAY
3	CHAIN PLATES	PORT & STARB'D - OPTIONAL
4	TURNBUCKLES	PORT & STARB'D - OPTIONAL
5	DECK BLOCKS	PORT & STARBOARD
6	MOORING CLEAT	
7	HALLIARD CLEATS	PORT & STARBOARD
8	BOW CHOCK	
9	SHEET TRAVELER	
10	TILLER STRAP	FORWARD
11	TILLER STRAP	AFT
12	RUDDER PINTLES	UPPER & LOWER
13	SCREW GUDGEONS	UPPER & LOWER
14	SHEET BLOCK	ON TRAVELER
15	SHEET BLOCK	ATTACHED TO WORM
16	WORM	ON BOOM
17	GOOSENECK	ON BOOM
18	GOOSENECK BAND	ON MAST
19	MAST EYE BOLT	
20	UPPER BAND	ON MAST
21	PEAK HALLIARD BLOCK	ON MAST BAND
22	PEAK HALLIARD BLOCK	ON BRIDLE
23	THROAT HALLIARD BLOCK	ON MAST
24	THROAT HALLIARD BLOCK	ON GAFF
25	TOGGLE	
26	CLAPPER	
27	GAFF JAWS	ONE TO RIGHT HAND ONE TO LEFT HAND
28	MAST HOOPS	FIVE REQUIRED
29	UPPER BOOM CROTCH BRACKET	COMBINATION CLEAT
30	LOWER BOOM CROTCH BRACKET	
31	BRASS PIN	TO HOLD CENTERBOARD UP
32	HEADSTAY	10'-4½" LONG FROM EYE BOLT TO HOLE IN STEMHEAD FITTING
33	SHROUDS (PORT & STARB'D) OPTIONAL EQUIPMENT	10'-10⅝" LONG FROM EYEBOLT TO HOLE IN CHAINPLATE
34	TILLER	

SAIL PLAN & DECK PLAN

THE ORIGINAL
BEETLE CAT BOAT

BUILT EXCLUSIVELY BY
CONCORDIA CO. INC.
SOUTH DARTMOUTH, MASSACHUSETTS
SCALE: 1" = 1'-0"   JULY 1947
SAIL PLAN Rev. 1963

on junior (and senior, to a lesser degree) training, sailing, and racing matters. Of equal importance, there is a boatyard that has the facilities and the sole rights to build the Beetles, and that is most anxious to see that the class continues. Concordia Company is always pleased to have interested parties visit the Beetle building project, to just watch the boats being built, or to get advice or parts for maintenance or repairs.

Beetles built twenty-five and more years ago are racing against new ones and are changing hands at prices higher than their original cost. Children are sailing the same Beetle that their father learned to

sail in. Grandfathers who sailed Beetles are giving their grandchildren Beetles, feeling that the boats are fine training ships, that the care and responsibility of such a boat is valuable experience, and that when the boat is available they themselves can again enjoy an evening sail or two.

Leo Telesmanick, who has personally been building the Beetles for thirty-seven years, tells me that old John Beetle, who started the class, told him this: "As long as people continue to get married and have children, Beetles will be built and sailed." I, personally, feel that John Beetle was a very wise man.

Beetles racing on Narragansett Bay. (Concordia Company)

It is interesting for me to realize that for several generations the Beetles and Howlands have had interests in common. Both families had homes on Clark's Point, which forms the western arm of New Bedford harbor. Both had connections with the whaling business. The Beetles were builders of the famous Beetle whaleboats. The Howlands were owners and captains of whaleships — one, by the way, being named *Concordia*. My own father's first job was at the Beetle Boat Yard and his first craft, a 30′ double-ended Block Island boat, was built at Beetle's.

I myself landed in the yacht brokerage and design business soon after leaving school. We first had an office at 50 State Street, Boston, and for our company Ray Hunt and I used the name Concordia. In the early thirties, when we were getting started, conditions were rather different from what they are now. During one of our most successful months we actually sold a ten-meter boat. The sales price was twenty-two hundred dollars. We were paying our wonderful Miss Shine thirteen dollars a week, and she cleaned our office, answered the phone, wrote all our letters, kept the books, tended to the files, and all. Thompson's Spa was serving a lunch for twenty cents, although they were cutting their pie in five pieces rather than four. In those years Miss Ruth Beetle and her sister, Miss Clara Beetle, were running the Beetle

Cat Boat business, which their father, John Beetle, had started in 1921. Leo Telesmanick, then in his teens, was working as apprentice for John Baumann, son-in-law of Charles Beetle, the whaleboat builder, who was actually building the 12′ Beetle Cats. The two of them, with the help of another boy in the summer, were producing some twenty-five boats each year. At first the price was $225, but in the thirties it was $250. One of the first little fleets went to Duxbury, Massachusetts, and Leo tells me that being a little late on their schedule, the boats had to be finished on the truck on the way to Duxbury.

The Misses Beetle followed the old-time sales policy of direct sales from builder to owner. This had some real advantages as well as obvious limitations. However, it worked then and still works today. In spite of this policy, some of us who really liked the Beetle Cats were allowed a five-dollar commission if we brought in a new customer. Not much profit, but real satisfaction just the same.

In 1941 Concordia moved to its present location at South Wharf in Padanaram. This old stone wharf had seen the building of many schooners and other vessels, and was last owned by Colonel Green, the son of the famous "Witch of Wall Street" — Hetty — who herself was a Howland. To this day I do not know how I was fortunate enough to complete my dream of ownership, because all

A Beetle Cat regatta on Buzzards Bay. (Concordia Company)

other Green property and assets were, as a matter of policy, kept or given away. The production of Beetles came practically to a stop during the years of World War II. Concordia's principal business changed from selling and designing to storage and repair of yachts. Uncle Sam, by some strange coincidence, sent me to Dartmouth, England, after which my home town is named and from which many of my ancestors came.

On my return in 1946 I found that the Misses Beetle's brother Carl had become involved with the building of Beetle Catboats, but was now thinking in terms of fiberglass construction rather than wood. This was not in my opinion a change for the better. I pleaded with Carl many times to build a few more wooden Beetles, or at least finish up his four half-built boats. My arguments carried no weight with him. However, he finally said to me, "If you think the wooden Beetle is so good, you can buy the whole bit and do with it what you will." His only stipulation was that I call them "Wooden Beetles." So, this was fine, we agreed upon a price for the moulds, tools, partly finished hulls, and other stock on hand.

Carl himself did go seriously into the fiberglass boat business. He was one of the first, if not the very first, to do so. His catboats, which he called B. B. Cats, had much the same dimensions and were similar in general shape to the Wooden Beetles. There were fundamental differences, however. The cockpit was longer and the deck shorter; more seating space, but less protection from rough waters. The rig was marconi, with aluminum, not wooden, spars. The weight of Carl's boat was less than the original, and the distribution of these weights came in different places. This is not obvious but does upset a lot of sailing qualities. From my point of view, the B. B.'s were never a real success, although they were well and strongly built. Production lasted a few years, but Carl himself moved from New Bedford to Fall River, and his production changed from boats to other items.

At the time that Concordia acquired the wooden Beetle, it was my intention to build a few of these boats each winter when other yard jobs were slack. It did not work out this way, however. We soon received more Beetle orders than we could possibly produce with our present set-up. Right at this point my friend and boatyard competitor, Palmer Scott, also of New Bedford, came to me with a most opportune and workable suggestion. He told me that some months back he himself had tried to buy the Beetle Catboat business, but that at that time Carl did not want to sell. Palmer had then asked Phil Rhodes to design for him a similar boat, the Wood Pussy, which was already in production. Leo Telesmanick was working for Palmer and was in charge of this Wood Pussy project, which was of conventional wood construction, oak, cedar, etc. Palmer offered to have Leo build the Beetles for Concordia to sell as well as the Wood Pussy for himself. And so it was that Scott did build the Beetles for Concordia for a number of years until in his operation his work became mostly fiberglass. As a matter of interest, Scott did, over a period of some ten years, build a very impressive number of Wood Pussys, first of wood and later of fiberglass. Personally, I never liked the tall marconi mast, placed way up in the eyes of the relatively fine bow of these cats, but the class, in spite of my opinion, was popular on Long Island Sound and elsewhere, and production continued until Scott's retirement about 1960.

In 1959 we moved the actual building of the Beetles from Scott's yard on Clark's Point to Padanaram. Strangely enough, Scott's yard was on almost the same spot as where Beetle had had his shop. A coincidence also was the fact that Concordia's building sheds were located on former Howland land on Smith Neck. This property on Smith Neck Road is just north of the property owned for many years by Hetty Green, and later Colonel Green.

With the move from Clark's point to Smith Neck came Leo Telesmanick, who continues to be in charge of building Beetles. The year 1973 will make for him more than forty years with the Beetles, a class which had its fiftieth anniversary in 1970.

In 1969 my brother and I sold the Concordia Company to William Pinney, formerly of Martha's Vineyard. Beetle policy, however, continues to be the same as in the past. The aim is to build a good wood boat, of strictly one-design construction, and to sell it from builder to buyer. Since 1921 only a few changes have been made in the construction of the Beetle. The earliest Beetle Cats were built exactly as the whaleboat had been. Both were built right side up, that is the keel and skeg were built first. Then the stem and garboard followed the keel. Next the planking was built upwards, board on board. Only when the planking was completed was the framing added. Now, for uniformity's sake, the hulls are framed over a mold and then planked. The stems are now laminated and not built up of natural crooks. The fastenings are now screws and not nails. Design and hardware remain the same.

In 1948 I assembled a small booklet on the original Beetle Catboats. I asked Lois Darling to draw for me several sketches which are reproduced here. I also asked for comments from a number of the Beetle fleets. One of these I quote from below, feeling Mr. Richard S. Borden, from Westport, Massachusetts, has really put his finger on the basic reason for a Beetle Cat.

"What we needed," Mr. Borden wrote, "was a small boat, since we maintain them ourselves, one with plenty of room, since we all have families, but a boat fast enough to buck four-knot tide and rugged enough to sail in the open ocean. There is only one boat that has these qualifications, the Beetle. We use Beetles for almost everything. We go on picnics, troll for bass and bluefish, spend leisurely hours going far up river, or off shore, sometimes as far as Hen & Chickens. On Sunday afternoons we hold races; sometimes as many as three or four. There is a great deal of competition, and afterwards much time is spent in hashing and rehashing each move. The enthusiasm with which we started has increased rather than diminished. Often we hold family races in which two or three children from five to ten years of age help crew each boat. These children are well on the way to becoming competent seamen. For safety, economy and fun, you can't beat these little boats."

Chapter 9

RESTORATION OF KIDDIE KAT
by John C. Freeburg

The life of many an old catboat has been extended far beyond normal expectation by timely and imaginative curative action. Owners of old boats faced with a major restoration can take heart from John C. Freeburg's account of "bulling his way through" the technical problems in three major restorations on his 42-year-old Anderson-built Kiddie Kat. John describes the technical problems involved in renewing the cockpit deck, reconstructing the mast step and its supports, and building a new boom.

John M. Leavens

If any one is interested in technical problems relative to the "preservation and restoration of ancient catboats so that they may remain a valuable asset in a civilization fast losing touch with ancient artifacts," we have, as usual, bulled our way through a few of these problems the past few springs.

RENEWING THE COCKPIT DECK

The loudest complaint coming from *Kiddie Kat* one fall was a somewhat shaky mounting for the steering mechanism, said steering mechanism being a huge worm-gear device coupled to a yoke on the head of the rudder post. A preliminary survey showed that sawing out a section of cockpit deck on each side of the steering post would give access to the supporting timbers. These could be replaced (easily?) and the cutaway area of cockpit decking replaced without too much mental or physical effort. Naturally, with such an accurate preliminary survey, we didn't start our repair work until late May when the breezes finally went balmy.

Cutting out the decking on either side of the steering box was the only easy job from there on in.

For background, the cockpit sole and main cabin deck had been fiberglassed somewhere around 1958 or 1959 in the early days of fiberglass. The glass had been apparently laid on over the original oiled narrow-strip decking and never did really stick because it was not laminated onto clean, oil-free wood. Since buying *Kiddie Kat* in 1960, we have been tacking and patching this deck. Tearing off a little of this around the steering box showed a real mess underneath. The only solution seemed to be to rip out the complete cockpit sole, benches, steering gear, gas tanks, engine hatches, etc. This proved to be a long job for saws, sabre-saws, chisels, pry bars, hacksaws, etc. As might be expected, the deck carlings (beams) had also been attacked by creeping paralysis here and there. Some of these had to be replaced. Others were patched or doubled up. Tearing out the cockpit like this also allowed easy inspection of the hull frames, floor timbers, and keel. A couple of frame areas were

Rebuilding the cockpit. Several carlins are in place.

cut out and sister frames installed but most were in good shape. All of the above were refastened and the whole area absolutely drowned in a mixture of Cuprinol and linseed oil.

At this point we had to decide what to do (after replacing the heavy timbering supporting the steering column with good white oak) about the cockpit deck, or sole if you wish. The sensible way would have been to nail two layers of ½-inch plywood (two half-inch layers would take the crown or curve of the deck while a 1-inch single layer would be too stiff). Then fiberglass could be laminated onto clean wood and all hands would be happy forever after. This seemed like the coward's way out and we reasoned that an oiled, narrow-strip, deck had been the right thing in 1927, so why not now?

Research showed that originally these narrow-strip, caulked and oiled decks had been either Eastern white pine, Douglas fir, or teak (on millionaires' boats). Clear Eastern pine is just about as extinct as short hair at Harvard. Teak for our income is *very* extinct. Clear fir I could only find in stair-tread material. The end result was the use of 1" x 12" fir ripped to 1" x 1¾" strips. Each strip was hand planed to a slight bevel on one edge as boat hull planking would be. Our dearly beloved boatyard proprietor, whom I hate passionately but have to be agreeable to or with, suggested that this sort of deck just had to be caulked with polysulfide rubber (fake rubber) compound. He suggested that the seams should not be caulked with cotton first but be filled with this fake rubber stuff. Having read technical advice from the revered Catboat Association Bulletins and the various boat-

ing magazines over the past several years, we fell for the sticky black mess. This meant that every deck strip, after first coating the original plank with Cuprinol on the bottom surface before ripping, had to be coated with a special primer on the edge and ends before laying. Replacing and doubling the deck beams took time and required hand ripping to a template with the correct curve, etc. Framing-in the hatches, manhole plate, etc, in our rather large cockpit took more time. While all this preliminary wood work was going on, I succeeded in convincing my good wife and the two oldest girls that things would move a lot faster if they would start to use the Kuhl's Rub-R-Seam glop in the seams as I would lay the deck strips just ahead of them. So I drilled and counterbored for the galvanized ring nails. Somebody mentioned a caulking gun for this caulking job. Maybe it would work but we didn't find the right nozzle shape, or something, and our beloved yard proprietor suggested that the only way was to mask all the seams with masking tape and fill them with the time-honored putty knife. This the girls did to the best of their ability. I have two pictures (color) of my wife pushing black sticky rubber compound into deck seams. She is complete with black rubber compound on her hands, knees, elbows, and where she happened to sit down on some. These could be made available if deemed of historical or technical value. At any rate, we finally finished after the pirate who runs our boatyard had sold us almost four cans (about 1 quart each) of rubber and three, one-pint cans of primer at $9.95 per can of compound and $3.25 per can of primer. The deck was then soaked a couple of times with a mixture of raw linseed oil and clear Cuprinol. We can't seem to learn if this is right for oiled decks but after several weeks our decks look just as stained and dirty as anyone else's oiled decks, so we figured we've been successful.

The material cost, considering lumber, nails, deck plugs for nailheads, compound, and primer, came to about $150; blood, sweat, and tears about $5,000. Of course, this is a large cockpit. Had we not been smitten with the "preserve the catboat" obsession, we could probably have put in fiberglass over plywood decks for one-half the price and one-third the labor. At any rate no one can accuse us of not following tradition unless they analyze the seam compound. (Really, we don't claim this as an attribute.) We don't really know if the deck leaks either as we don't sleep under the cockpit.

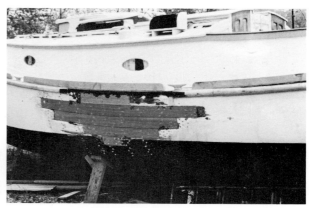

Sawn replacement frames were inserted from out-side, new butt blocks were put in place, and all new

wood was soaked with Cuprinol. Then the new planks completed the job.

RECONSTRUCTING THE MAST STEP AND ITS SUPPORTS

As a sequel to this story, I had known that the mast step area needed attention but figured the next year would be soon enough. A couple of weeks later, Charlie, my oldest son, and I were out in a moderate breeze when we noticed water where it shouldn't be, like above the cabin sole. The mast step had split or shifted and planks were being pushed outward. Obviously, my next repair job was cut out for me.

Examination showed that the mast step had sheared its meager fastening from a repair done in 1952. At the time of this previous repair, a new knee had been installed and the mortise for the step had been cut into it. The frames had been cut off to allow for fitting this knee but that was it. None of them had been re-mortised into the knee. Essentially, the mast step was simply a knee spiked into the stem and keel with no supporting frames or ribs. The spikes had died a slow death and the step in the knee began to move. The repair consisted of tearing off the planking in the forefoot area, both sides, to be able to *see* the damage. The wood was solid, so 10-inch lag screws were driven through the knee, in which the step mortise was located, to refasten it. Then a 2½-inch-thick oak saddle member was fitted. It dropped down two inches on either side of the knee and was spiked and mortised into the knee. The mast wood was cut back to allow for the additional step thickness. Sister frames were installed alongside the old frames and were also mortised into the knee and the new saddle member. The lousy part was re-planking the forefoot which had been de-planked

six to eight feet back from the stem and included the wide garboard at the point of its worse twist. Not having steaming facilities, I thought first of replanking with one-inch-square glued and edge-nailed strips. This was fine for three strips, but it became impossible to edge nail with the old planking in place beyond this. I resorted to reasonably narrow planking for the rest of one side (Philippine mahogany) pushed into place with props, levers, and clamps. One side was planked easily, but I apparently used a brittle cross-grained piece for the other side and split every piece in trying to horse it into place. Time was growing short, so I used the coward's way out and used two layers of one-half-inch plank with glue between for this side. No problem to date.

BUILDING A NEW BOOM

Now, about the boom. The old one, so far as I know the last of the original spars, was in poor shape with splits and cracks all over. We built a new one out of Eastern spruce with a few small knots. We laminated 2″ x 6″ boards together after first scarf-gluing 18-foot lengths together to get three planks, 2″ x 6″ by 30 feet long. This was roughed out to octagon form and then planed round by hand to 5″ diameter in the middle, tapering to 4″ at the mast end, and 3½″ at the clew end, as per the old boom. We capped off the clew end with a carved mahogany star. Even though solid, it is lighter than the old fir boom and gives us all new spars (since 1966). With a new sail (Mills) last year we are beginning to get that "high-class" feeling but try to soft-peddle it lest those seekers of unpaid bills descend all at once!

Chapter 10

RESTORATION OF THE CATBOAT FRANCES
by John P. Brewer

John P. Brewer describes in detail a more extensive restoration for museum display purposes of the 72-year-old Wilton Crosby catboat Frances *now in the Mystic Seaport collection.*

John M. Leavens

Visitors to Mystic Seaport in the 1960's had the good fortune to see a pretty white catboat gracing the waterfront near the schooner *Bowdoin.* However, she deteriorated badly and had to be retired in 1968. Late in 1969, the Marine Historical Society decided to rebuild her and the Catboat Association, at its annual meeting, voted $500 toward the cost of the restoration work. Fred Cousins of Noank did the restoration work and Maynard Bray was in charge for Mystic Seaport. During the progress of the work he kept a photographic record of what was done.

When you remember the restoration of the catboat *Frances,* think of Fred Cousins painstakingly whittling and gluing plugs for each of the old nail and screw holes in her planking.

Or think of Fred faced with such difficulty in fitting new oak ribs to the 70-year-old lady that he had to forge his own special tools for the job.

Or think of him day after day working to strip the many coats of paint from her — white, green, and gray, and at the base in some places, varnish. "We used the torch and mechanical scrapers," Fred said, "but everything we could get loose, like the beaded cabin staving, we sent to a furniture dip

place. At one point we were thinking of cutting the whole boat up into eight pieces and putting them all in the tank. We spent as much time removing paint as we did on the wood work."

Restoration of the *Frances* into Mystic Seaport's newest exhibit cost five months' work and $6,000 — not including materials, which the Seaport produced — to make her as authentic as possible. However, *Frances* was not in sailing condition even after this expenditure, because as Maynard Bray observed, the object of the restoration work was to retain as much of the original material as possible, yet build in lasting strength for an inside exhibit.

Here's what the work included:

NEW OAK FRAMES
For this job Fred needed the help of Bob Morse, a local boatbuilder. "I took one frame at a time so as not to lose her shape. We steamed each frame and then had to tuck the ends in under the clamp, as fast as we could. As far as we could, we put the frames in the same place, so that meant knocking fittings out and gluing in plugs. We fastened while the steamed frame was still hot and the fastenings would draw it into shape. We worked with

Frances in 1960 at Mystic Seaport before restoration. Whaler Charles W. Morgan *in left background; Admiral MacMillan's Arctic-exploring schooner* Bowdoin *at right. (Louis S. Martel, Mystic Seaport)*

The interior of Frances' *cabin before restoration showing peeling paint. (Louis S. Martel, Mystic Seaport)*

71

Tying the staving and cockpit deck together. (M. E. Bray, Mystic Seaport)

Enough of Frances' *cockpit decking remained to be duplicated in new wood. (Louis S. Martel, Mystic Seaport)*

Fred Cousins, who restored Frances, *used the torch and mechanical scrapers but "everything we could get loose we sent to the furniture dip place — things like the beaded cabin staving." (Louis S. Martel, Mystic Seaport)*

72

The after end of Frances' rudder was rebuilt. This view illustrates the general size and shape of the underslung rudder of a counter-stern cat. It is smaller and entirely different in profile from the more common outboard, barn-door rudder found in cats of the transom-stern model. (Louis S. Martel, Mystic Seaport)

a bucking iron and twisting tool I made especially for this; it saved our lives."

However, in refastening, Fred used bronze screws or bronze nails clinched instead of the original iron nails or later refastening that included screws.

"There was a very low headroom in the cabin," he said, "less than four feet, and with the centerboard case, it was some hard to work in. But we numbered the planks inside and outside so I could call, say, for putting a fastening in the bottom of No. 6 plank. It worked pretty good."

NEW BEADED STAVING IN SOME PLACES

"I had to make my own molding plane for this — two of them," Fred said. "The chips didn't clear very good from them, but if I'd worked it a bit it would have been better. The joiner work was all beaded by hand as far as we could tell."

REFASTEN THE COCKPIT RAIL CAP AND FIT OARLOCKS

"The rail cap fastenings were iron and were gone completely," Fred said. "I remember when I was told in Maine that an iron-fastened boat is good for 20 years. We found evidence she was refastened once with nails and another time with screws. Oarlocks were pretty standard 70 years ago when she was built. She never had an engine. But the oarlocks had been removed and a piece fitted in."

REPLACE THE GUARD RAILS

"The guard rails were beat up so bad we never could have used them," Fred said. "She had rubbed a few pilings in her life; those rails were not banged by dinghies — they were gouged."

REFASTEN THE DECK

"Aft, she had short deck beams," Fred said, "and some had dropped off completely and lay in the bottom of the boat. The fastenings, iron again, were 100 percent gone."

RECANVAS THE CABIN TOP AND DROP THE COCKPIT FLOOR

"We tore up the cockpit floor because the original was four inches lower," Fred said. "Someone had raised it so it would be self bailing."

INSTALL A NEW STERNPOST

"The iron fastenings had split the sternpost all to pieces," Fred said, "but it wasn't a tremendous job."

One of the important considerations in the restoration was that Frances be as "original" as possible. She measures 20 feet, 10 inches overall; 19 feet, 5 inches on the waterline. Her beam is 10 feet and she draws 2 feet with her board up. Frances has a high bow and a counter stern with a tucked-in-under transom rudder instead of the barn-door variety often seen on cats. Frances was built by Wilton Crosby in Osterville, Mass., in 1900, and is considered a prime example of the Cape Cod cat.

"She was built as a party boat," Fred said, "and used to take people out for afternoon sails. She wasn't a workboat because she has a large cockpit — but no fish well. And she carries less sail than would be found on a racer."

Frances was first owned by Shields Gurley of Nantucket. Later she was acquired by the Burnett

Restoration completed in June, 1970, Frances *returns to Mystic Seaport. Note the crab support for the boom just aft of the mast hole and the oval fixed ports typical of early catboats. (Louis S. Martel, Mystic Seaport)*

family who gave her in 1959 to Mystic Seaport where she was exhibited in the water. In 1968 she was put into storage until Fred could begin work on her.

Frances, restored, is on exhibit in the converted spar shed near the *Joseph Conrad,* heeled down so the inside of the cabin may be seen. Here she is protected from sun, wind, rain, and snow and should last indefinitely.

Fred, 52, a native of Blue Hill, Maine, has leased his yard — Eldridge Boat Yard, Inc. — since 1969 and has rehabilitated two other Seaport boats, including the New Haven oyster sloop. His 20-foot by 36-foot shop has had full-time work.

Two things stand out from his work on *Frances:* the weakness of the iron fastenings, and the hardiness of the cypress, especially the three-quarter-inch planking.

"I learned a lot about the rusting of iron," Fred said. "They go away to nothing. It proves that acid in the oak eats fastenings faster than other kinds of wood. The original nails were cut nails,

and the nail heads were covered with beeswax — it used to be the standard method of plugging holes. So we had to punch them out or try to work them free. You had to be very tender with them, but we thought that the cypress planking was worth saving if we could."

That was the reason for the plugs whittled out of cypress and glued in with epoxy — as many as 24 plugs in half a butt. "We'd roll the boat back and forth two-three times a day so we could work up," he said.

But apart from the fastening holes, the cypress wood "is as good as the day it was put in."

"The centerboard we did not replace," Fred said. "They decided it would not be a water-display boat. The centerboard was somewhat questionable being old, but it looked all right and we didn't dig into it too greatly.

"If you put it in the water you've got to paint it every year. But if you put it on a land display, the paint is good for five years. If these old boats are worth saving, it's worth doing well."

Chapter 11

MAINTAINING A CATBOAT
by Oscar C. Pease

Vanity, a 20-foot Manuel Swartz Roberts cat, was built as a working cat in Edgartown for Oscar Pease's father in 1929. It has been sailed ever since, winter and summer, first by the father and, in more recent years, by the son. In the wintertime, Vanity is a bay scalloper towing as many as eight heavy metal dredges astern under power. In summer, Vanity is a party cat, rigged for bluefishing or beach parties under sail or power.

Vanity is kept afloat year around and hauled twice a year for maintenance and painting. Oscar does his own work. As a result, Vanity is immaculate at all times. Part of the secret lies in the color pattern Oscar uses. The topsides are the traditional white but the cabin house top, cockpit and deck are done in continental buff. Light wash colors and careful washdowns with salt water and mop after each run help keep the boat looking pristine. As might be expected of one who has had more than forty years' experience in one catboat, not to mention a boyhood spent in earlier cats, and who has worked professionally in a yard (Norton and Easterbrooks of Edgartown) ministering to cats and other types of boats, Oscar has accumulated tricks and knowledge of boat maintenance that represent the experience of generations of catboat sailors.

Herein, Oscar shares his wealth of experience. Much of what he has to say is uncommon commonsense that is applicable not alone to catboats but to boats of all kinds.

John M. Leavens

A few observations on catboat maintenance and repair, based on my experience both in keeping *Vanity* in condition and working between seasons in Norton and Easterbrooks yard may be of interest and help to other catboat owners.

PAINT

Perhaps the single most important factor in catboat maintenance is paint. Not only does paint give a boat a smart appearance, it also protects the boat's surfaces from moisture that can cause rot. A knowledge of the forces at work that affect paint is important to any boatowner whether he does his own work or has it done for him.

This past winter, *Vanity's* topsides were in very good shape up to about the first of February. That is when we began to have our harder weather here on Martha's Vineyard. It really got much colder at this time. We were down to around 20 degrees before then, but this much cold didn't seem to bother *Vanity*. However, when it got down to 10 degrees and later 5 degrees, along in there, the effects of the frost started to show up, with the paint beginning to peel off the topsides. It is nothing unusual. *Vanity* has always peeled, but the fact of peeling does raise two questions: "What happened?" and "What can be done about it?"

Two factors are responsible, in my opinion:

Vanity in summer rig. Oscar Pease's catboat Vanity *is shown under sail rigged as a summer party boat, with after-wheel steering. (Nellie Pease)*

moisture and extreme cold. When the frost gets into the wood, the frost crystals expand as they freeze and contract as they thaw. Between thawing and freezing, the moisture penetrates so deep into the wood that eventually it pushes the paint right off. There probably will always be a certain amount of paint lifting where fresh water gets in, even in the absence of frost. This can happen in the summer months. But real serious damage to the paint is done by the action of the frost, and anything that can prevent frost from forming is helpful.

I use *Vanity* all year around. Except when she is hauled for painting, she is in the water. Being in the water all the time, *Vanity* absorbs moisture. Naturally, I have a problem with my washboards, because hauling the scallop drags does knock the paint off. You just can't keep it there. Each time a scallop dredge bangs her topsides, a small chip of paint flakes off and an avenue for moisture is opened up. On damp days, moisture condenses on almost any surface that lacks good ventilation. So, as the winter sets in with its freezing temperatures, frost gets on the wood surfaces and even into the wood itself. Moisture not only condenses on surfaces, it also penetrates in back of the bulkheads and underneath the decks and works its way through the wood to peel paint and varnish off the exterior surfaces. Varnish doesn't lift quite the same way that paint does. Varnish will lift if there

is more or less of a continuation of moisture that gets in behind it through a seam or a crack. If this happens, the wood gets to a sort of dead point where the varnish doesn't seem to have anything to grab on to and hold.

Vanity's cabin house roof has been fiberglassed over so that no moisture can leak down through the roof. Any moisture that settles on the inside of the cabin roof must be a result of condensation. Yet *Vanity's* cabin when the cabin roof overhead was the fact is that on real cold days, I've been in so thick with frost you could scoop it right off. When it isn't frost, it's sweat or beads of water that stay there until you can get dry air circulating long enough to dry it out.

Salt is a natural preservative of wood and it doesn't do any damage to a boat when it lies in the bilges or on exposed surfaces. The old whaler *Charles W. Morgan* at Mystic Seaport has loose "ice cream salt" in her bilges as a preservative, so that if rain, or fresh water from any source, should leak down through the deck or around the mast and be trapped in an area where it will not run off easily, the salt makes the fresh water salty and thus preserves the wood and checks dry rot.

If a boat can be kept well painted with no cracks, which is a hard thing to do, you can help guard against moisture. These days a lot of people fiberglass their decks. That is probably a good thing. For the most part, it keeps the fresh water at least from filtering down below decks. When you have a wood boat with the sun pulling on its seams, there is bound to be some opening in her exposed surfaces. If you can get fiberglass on these surfaces, it makes one continuous sheet and eliminates the rainwater problem. By the same token, if the hull were fiberglassed — and it is, of course, quite expensive to get this work done — it could probably eliminate the problem of rust spots, particularly on the topsides. Nails, after so many years, do lose their galvanizing and tend to rust. With fiberglass, you would have a good, smooth topside. That probably would help eliminate the peeling of paint. When a boat that is used only in the summer and stored in the winter gets to be 20-years old, rust spots begin to show. There are fewer rust-spot problems with a boat that is kept in the water the year round. Any boat that is built with iron nails that are galvanized will only last so long. Salt gradually gets in on the nail, and eventually the nail gets to the point where the galvanizing gives up and the iron starts to rust.

I have taken out several of these rusty nails from *Vanity* and replaced them with Everdur screws. It is quite a trick to pull them. I take a narrow chisel and cut under each side of the nail enough to get a sharp pointed nail puller under it and pull it that way. After putting the screw in we used to use wood dough to fill in the gouge hole, which we smoothed off afterwards before painting. Nowadays, fiberglass putty is better. It doesn't shrink like wood dough and you can paint over it. In fact, you can even put paint on when the wood is wet and it will stick. You can't do this with anything else.

Some kinds of wood are more susceptible than others to paint-lifting action. Moisture doesn't seem to bother cedar as much as it does other woods. There is a top strake of cypress in *Vanity* that apparently still has a lot of sap in it 38 years after *Vanity* was built. The first place the paint leaves is right where that sapwood is. We tried to overcome peeling paint by burning all the paint off the boat. Then we primed and painted it carefully, but the paint still flakes off this cypress top strake when the weather gets very cold. I suppose the sapwood may be so hard that the paint doesn't grasp it as it does a softer wood.

Years ago, most boats were made of cedar. Cedar has a lot of holding power for paint. Some boats are built with hard pine for the three or four strakes down from the top strake because a boat can take more abuse with hard pine than with cedar. Hard pine is a hard wood. Cedar is softer and shows up dents. It is always harder to burn paint off cedar than it is on cypress or hard pine. When you burn a boat planked with hard pine, the paint comes off just like water off a duck's back. Oak is a hard wood that can hold anything. It is even hard enough to hold fiberglass. There is apparently an acid in oak that seems to assist anything like paint and fiberglass. The best wood is teak. When you use teak you don't have any problems of freshwater rot. If you paint teak, it's okay. If you don't, it still won't rot and it is not affected by moisture.

Generally, the decks up forward along the sides of *Vanity's* cabin don't present a paint-lifting problem to the same degree as in and around the cockpit. Of course, with any catboat there is the problem of dead air space behind the cockpit stave work and under the deck. On *Vanity*, when the outside of the washboard down near the deck gets wet, I practically need a drought here on the Vineyard to find a dry spell long enough and dry enough to get

Manuel Swartz Roberts, 1881-1963, builder of Vanity, *stands in the doorway to his boatshop (now The Old Sculpin Art Gallery) in Edgartown, Massachusetts, August, 1954. (Clair Birch)*

her dried out so she can be painted. I have drilled 1¼″ holes through the stave work that I block up with cork to keep the dirt out, as I use her for working in the winter months. I always pull these corks out in the summer. This provides ventilation for that dead air space because the cockpit deck doesn't go up above the timbers and there is an air space of 1¼″ to 1½″ in which air can circulate. For the best air circulation, the cabin should be wide open. That, of course, gives the entire boat better circulation. Naturally this is difficult to do in the winter months.

One place that is particularly vulnerable to moisture on a boat is the bottom. Even when the bilges are drained there is always a good deal of moisture in this part of the boat, more so than others, and the result is that the paint tends to leave the bottom during the winter months.

Naturally, if a boat is hauled and stored in a building for the winter it would have less exposure to moisture than a boat that is kept in the water all year around. Consequently, she would be less apt to have the paint free from her, unless she was completely soaked or saturated when she was laid up and no adequate provision was made at that time for ventilation and circulation of drying air. In laying up a boat in covered storage, it would help to get good air circulation if the engine hatch were taken off and the engine area were left wide open. Of course, in a building, there isn't too much force to move and circulate the air like there is out-doors, but if there were some means of keeping the temperature above the freezing point then there wouldn't be any problem of frost getting in to lift the paint. Storage in a heated building, or use of a heating element with a thermostatic control on board, would keep a stored boat dry in the winter months and also help prevent frost from forming.

As for storing boats outdoors, old-timers will tell you it is all right for boats to be covered up during the winter months, but just as soon as it starts to get warm at all, the covers should be taken off. Probably around the first of May is the best time to take the cover off. It doesn't do to keep a boat covered out in the hot sun, because the sun will bake down on it through the tarpaulin and really raise the temperature. If there is any dampness, the moisture will steam right down into the fibers of the wood. Nothing can ruin a wood hull any faster.

In March we get high winds, which seem to have more of a drying force than winds at other times of the year. Usually when a boat is stored outside, the bottom is painted with linseed oil to keep the wood from shrinking and drying out. Linseed oil has the virtue that it can be put on even over copper paint. Come spring you paint right over it.

When I was in the service I had *Vanity* up in my mother's yard covered over with canvas for 41 months. Fortunately, a neighbor had a big tree in the next yard, so in the summer *Vanity* was in the shade. It apparently didn't do *Vanity* any harm to be covered up like that for that length of time.

When I got back, one noticeable thing was the effect of the moisture on her bottom. We had been using a heavy grade of copper bottom paint and over the years it had built up quite a thickness. When I got back from the service, this paint hung off *Vanity's* bottom like leaves off a tree. It looked awful so I took a broom and brushed off what was

loose and what would come off readily. Then I took a blow torch and burned the rest off. As far as I could find out, that was the first time anyone had burned off the bottom of a catboat around Edgartown. In later years, this has been done quite frequently with beneficial results.

Some of the paint had peeled off the coaming, the decks, and such. I had laid her up in October, 1942, and some of the paint had come off naturally by then, but all things considered, her topsides and deck weren't in too bad shape when I returned in February, 1946. I burned her right off from the curb to the bottom of the keel. Then I put on three coats of paint. First, I painted her right from the washboard to the keel with red lead, and then I added two coats on her topsides. At that time, they claimed red lead was the best thing for under-coating. Of course, her sides and bottom seams had opened up, and I must have put in a quart of seam compound to fill them. Nowadays, the new syn-thetics are taking the place of the traditional seam compounds. Some people talk about polysulphate, others polysulphide. I don't know the difference between them, if, in fact, there are two separate synthetic substances. Polysulphide is the most com-mon name, but whatever the name (and I'll call it polysulphide) it comes in two forms: as a plastic material with a catalyst or activator, and ready mixed in tubes that can be used in a gun the same as painters' common caulking compound. Some of the bedding compounds put out by the Dolphinite people come in tubes, the same way. Compound is a lot easier to handle that way, because you don't have to bother mixing the ingredients. One vari-ety is called Polyseamseal elastic sealer. It comes in tubes and is made by Darnworth Incorporated of Simsbury, Connecticut. The ad for it says "bonds like glue; remains flexible." Polysulphide has a rub-bery, or maybe I should say rubberized, texture. It sticks to things, even to things you don't want it to stick to. You just gun the material on and smooth it with a putty knife. Warm water will dissolve the material before it has set, but a little acetone comes in handy in cleaning up your hands and your tools after you have used it.

In addition to making a line of polysulphide seam compound, Kuhls makes about the best ordin-ary deck compound. I don't know its formula. It has a putty base, only there seems to be more elas-ticity in it than there is in the common seam com-pounds that you hear so much about. International makes one brand and I guess Baltimore and all the

Vanity *in winter rig. Oscar Pease has removed* Vanity's *spars and sail, and has installed forward-wheel steering, a companionway enclosure, and a culling board. She is now ready for scalloping. (Edith Blake)*

other paint manufacturers have their own brands.

A number of boatyards away from here use polysulphide for a filler compound as a matter of course. I have used some at Norton and Easterbrooks on several boats, but mostly they have been transient jobs so I never saw the results of the application afterwards. This spring I used polysulphide for a filler in *Vanity's* deck. It stuck well to the new wood in filling the deck seams and did not show any signs of opening or checking during the hot summer weather.

We have a paint called SavCote advertised as a "liquid plastic coating" that comes in both white and "plasti-clear" and is said to resist salt, rust, and rot. The directions say that this paint can even fill a ¼″ seam. Well, you can't fill a ¼″ seam on deck, much less a seam overhead, by painting into the

seam. It would take forever. But we have used SavCote after filling the seams with polysulphide caulking. SavCote comes in cans and has an activator in a separate unit. You can use as much of this activator as you think you are going to need in proportion to the amount in the can. If you are going to use all of it, you dump in all the activator and use it up, but if you are only going to use part of it, you act accordingly. This particular brand requires the ingredients to be mixed together for five minutes. It states so in the directions. You have to mix by your watch for five minutes before you apply any of it where you are going to use it. So with the polysulphide caulking and this undercoat of paint made by SavCote, plus their anti-fouling paint, all of which have a plastic foundation, the combination actually makes a sheet of plastic. It worked

Oscar Pease sets scallop dredges from Vanity *in Katama Bay, Martha's Vineyard, February, 1965. (John M. Leavens)*

wonders on an Owens with a "rubber bottom" and practically made her tight.

The paint isn't very heavy to put on. In fact, it's very thin. The copper paint is just about the consistency of beet juice and looks like it. But it dries in about 15 to 20 minutes, so you can go right around the boat if you want to and give her a second coat as soon as you get her done the first time. SavCote has a setting-up factor that depends on the temperature. The warmer it is, the less time it takes to cure.

The plastic compounds are more expensive, say, than regular seam compounds, but I think they are worth the difference. If the directions are followed properly and if the compound is put on in proper form, I think it's well worth the extra effort and the price. I don't know of any disadvantages, except that it's awful messy stuff, but if you do get your hands into it you can clean them with acetone.

Prices vary for the polysulphide in tubes. A 16-ounce tube of Polyseamseal runs about $1.95. I have bought polysulphide from Sears Roebuck for about $7 for three tubes or about $2.35 a tube. A gun runs about $2.00 If you have a tube of polysulphide and use only a part, you can store it and use the rest later. It will harden in the nozzle but you can pick this hardened material out with a long nail and the rest will still be soft and usable.

Perhaps the use will determine which form of synthetic to apply. The tube variety is principally for caulking and spot sealing jobs. SavCote is thinner and is used to cover larger areas.

RECOVERING DECKS AND CABIN HOUSE TOPS

The traditional covering for decks and cabin house tops, of course, is canvas. However, the canvas that I have put on the tops of catboat cabins at Norton and Easterbrooks, over the last 15 or 20 years, doesn't seem to have the quality of fiber that canvas had years ago. It doesn't seem to last more than three to five years before it cracks and rots and has to be replaced. When I fiberglassed the top of

Vanity's cabin in 1962, I took off the original canvas that Manuel Swartz Roberts had put there 32 years earlier. I got down to bare wood before putting on the fiberglass.

Canvas will crack or paint will crack on canvas from overpainting or application of too many coats of paint. Actually, canvas should be just colored very lightly with the proper color of paint. It should be just colored enough so it looks decent. You shouldn't put on several coats of paint because it builds up, unless you are very handy at sandpapering and can sandpaper off as much as is put on. There is a different expansion-shrinkage coefficient for canvas than for paint, and if the paint is thick, the canvas gives underneath the paint. This movement between the two could cause the paint to split open and crack.

I burned the paint off my canvas one time with a blowtorch. It can be done without burning the canvas, but you really have to watch your procedure because you can make a mistake so easily. You have to work in moderate or light air, or no air at all, so you get more of an even heat. You must watch very closely because the concentration of heat can raise the canvas itself into a bubble. Then you can't get it back down again.

There are two different things to use in putting canvas on. There is a waterproof glue that can be used. There is also a type of bedding compound that can be applied to the wood before you set the canvas into it.

Nowadays, fiberglass is taking the place of canvas for decks and cabin house tops. Many consider fiberglass the ideal material for this purpose. However, fiberglass over common lumber involves certain risks, such as cracking and splitting open, because the wood has so much "come and go" with the dampness and drying out. Just this winter the top of my cabin split. Why, I don't know. It hadn't happened before, although the fiberglass covering has been on there seven years. Perhaps there were changes in the wood underneath that came about with age. The split in *Vanity's* cabin top was only a hairline crack but it wouldn't hold resin. I put some 1½" fiberglass tape over the crack. First I sanded through the paint and got down to fiberglass. Then I fiberglassed the tape in place, sanded it smooth, and painted over it.

If anybody were going to build a new cabin house top, they should use plywood as a base for the fiberglass. I think they will get much better results. Any exterior grade plywood will do. I have found it to be not too bad around water. It has a waterproof glue and that's the most important factor. Most cabin houses are crowned. If the plywood is thin enough it will conform to quite a bend. If the cabin doesn't have too much crown you could get by with ⅜" plywood. You wouldn't want to go any thicker than that. You could put on two layers of ¼". That would be plenty strong enough and you can easily handle the thinner plywood. It bends to conform lots easier than the thicker plywood does.

There isn't much maintenance to a fiberglass cabin top. If it gets scuffed and shows the fiberglass cloth, it may require painting over with a coat of resin. Sometimes the fiberglass cloth gets air bubbles under it. When this happens, you can sandpaper and cut through the cloth. The sandpaper takes hold of the bubble quicker than it does the stuck-down cloth. If you sandpaper too much, you will get a hole. The best thing to fill a hole is fiberglass body putty, such as is used in automobile paint shops.

Fiberglass has many other uses around a boat than covering decks and cabin tops. You can use it around the stave work where it joins the cockpit floor if you have a problem where it's leaking at that point. Fiberglass will seal things you can't seem to seal with anything else. It makes a better protection for plywood than paint alone. I've covered my engine hatch by sealing it with fiberglass cloth and resin. I put scallop baskets on there. They have dirt on the bottom and scrape around and usually take the paint off, but they don't bother the fiberglass.

MAINTAINING THE CENTERBOARD AND BOX ON A CATBOAT

Taking the centerboard out is the first and most important step in maintaining both it and the box. Most centerboards swing on a single pin at the bottom of the board. Mine has a patented hanger that permits it to hang on a pin at the top. Once the board is removed, maintaining it presents no special problem. The box, however, is another matter. I have a sponge on a stick 1½" wide, ⅜" thick, and about 6 feet long that I use in maintaining *Vanity's* centerboard box. The sponge is fastened with large tacks and is also tied with stout cord so that it forms a swab. I use this to swab the centerboard box. Below and outside the box, I have a bucket of copper bottom paint on the underside of the keel. I dip the swab through the box, dunk it in the kettle, and pull up, swabbing up and down as I go. By pulling up I don't get paint in my face.

I generally try to wait until the sun is directly overhead so I can see inside the box clearly and make sure what is being covered with paint. In my case the boat is hauled up in a north-south direction. Somewhere around noon the sun shines directly into the box so I can see what I'm doing. An electric light bulb would probably serve to do the same thing.

I paint the board and box once a year. I also paint the bottom about once a year, although sometimes it has been done twice. I use a cheaper grade of copper bottom paint for the box than for the bottom, because it isn't necessary to keep the box from fouling up. It doesn't make that much difference. The bottom paint I use is $11.95 a quart. What I use for the box is Baltimore Copper at about $3.60 a quart. I also paint the fish well with this same cheaper paint.

When the boat is hauled, I first do the topsides. Then I do the copper bottom painting. After that I do the box. I keep the centerboard in the water so it won't warp. It's warped enough as it is. I pull it inshore long enough to dry it off, paint it, and launch it again.

Every now and then someone will come up with the bright idea of taking the cap off the top, plugging the bottom, and then filling up the box with copper bottom paint. This is prohibitively expensive. Yet, when I came back from the war, during which time *Vanity* was hauled with the centerboard left in the box, I took a roofing board and nailed it with six-penny nails driven into the keel over the opening and put a couple of strands of caulking around the edges. Then I poured about three gallons of creosote into the box. It doesn't take as much with the board in as it would with the board out. The boat had been out of water for about four years, so I thought it would be a good time to do this because it would be dry and the creosote would go into the wood. It came out through the seams in the centerboard trunk inside the cabin, and the stains are still there now and that was more than 25 years ago. I left the creosote in there for two weeks, and when I got it out I don't think I got a gallon out of the three. The creosote dried so I could paint over it. In fact, you can add creosote to copper paint as a thinner so it doesn't have to dry very much.

Any old catboat sailor knows that the center-board box is the Achilles heel of a catboat. It ought to be painted at least once a year and more often in tropical waters. Painting keeps out the worms and adds years to any cat's life. My boat doesn't have a worm in her, and she's more than 40 years old.

ELECTROLYSIS AND CORROSION

Not long ago, supporting beams under the cockpit floor began to give away. I first noticed that the floor seemed to have a rubbery feeling under my feet and moved quite a bit. By standing in certain areas I could see the floor come away from the stave work. Before long I had to replace parts of the floor and the supporting beams. When I got the old flooring off, I found that there was some soft wood in the stem that was a little dozy; that is, soft or punky. It probably never got completely dried out, although I do have air holes underneath there for air to circulate, but when something gets wet aboard a boat, it doesn't get dried out unless the boat is hauled out and left out of the water for six months or more.

What had happened to the cockpit floor and its supporting beams was something else. Only some parts of the beams had gone bad. For the most part, the nails had rusted off, the wood had become poor, then the nails loosened their grip, and, from a general slackening up of the parts, the cockpit deck became weak. This was a result of electricity and its effect on wood.

Electricity that goes through a boat makes the lumber in her become very stringy and feel "furry." You don't find this so much in a boat without an engine. The effect of these electrical currents on the wood in a boat is somewhat similar to the electrolysis that erodes metal. Where does this electricity come from? Mostly it's caused or generated, maybe "escapes" is a better word, from the engine. Bolted down as it is, the engine sets up an action with the outside water through the propeller and shaft to form electricity, which, in turn, makes the wood sort of dead, soft, and spongey. It electrocutes the wood, you might say.

You can look for signs of trouble of this kind after 20 years. Probably in a boat you just use in the summer months may not have any problems like that. But electrocuted wood is different, and I've seen many examples of it in my work at Norton and Easterbrooks. You just have to replace wood when it gets badly affected by electricity. Rising costs in boatyards to some extent has been responsible for the search for new cost-saving materials, including fiberglass, stainless steel, Monel, and aluminum, but the search has also been stimulated by the need for materials that aren't subject to corrosion by electrolysis.

Fiberglass is too well known for me to talk about it.

Stainless steel is used extensively in place of other things, but for the most part, it's hard to work with. For instance, if you want to drill a piece of stainless at a point where you want to put an extra screw in and you try to drill it with a high-speed drill, you won't get anywhere. It's got to be drilled very slowly so your drill doesn't heat up. I've never used lubrication for the drill tip when drilling stainless steel. If you drill slowly, as you should, you won't need lubrication. However, I've seen some fellows try to drill stainless steel on a normal drill stand and burn the drill right up doing so; everything smoked up and the metal was discolored light blue.

Monel has a lot of copper in the alloy. It is used mostly in fabricated parts such as a tank or for propeller shafting. Monel is like stainless. It can be welded or soldered. Some use is made of Monel for fastenings, but mostly at Norton and Easterbrooks we use Everdur screws for fastenings. Everdur is a bronze with a lot of copper in it. It's subject to electrolysis, but rarely does it erode.

Aluminum is also coming into extensive use in boatbuilding. It is used chiefly for stanchions, spars, and masts. Aluminum boats, in particular, often have a great deal of trouble with electrolysis. A fellow down at Katama had an aluminum boat, and he had such problems that he had some kind of machine put aboard to counteract this electrolysis and give the boat cathodic protection, but he finally got rid of the boat and I don't know how successful he was in guarding against the effects of electrolysis.

There is a certain amount of electricity in any boat. You can't help it. However, boats nowadays are loaded with radios, depthsounders, radars, and what not which multiplies the normal electrical currents many times. All this electronic gear requires the addition of some form of cathodic protection against the electrolysis that would otherwise erode all bronze gear and fittings. On boats this usually takes the form of an addition of zinc at a strategic point to cause the electrical currents generated by the electronic gear to leave the boat at the point selected. The currents erode the added zinc instead of eating up bronze shafting, propellers, struts, and bolts. Incidentally, all wooden boats have a positive ground, while all steel boats have a negative ground. This has to be taken into account in hooking up the electrical system.

Chapter 12

CAT POWER
by Oscar C. Pease

We have all heard lately about various kinds of power — political power, black power, and love power. This article is about cat power, the auxiliary inboard or outboard gasoline engines and appurtenant gear used to propel catboats.

Catboats built before the turn of the century never had cat power. They depended exclusively on sails and, occasionally oars, for their propulsion. Then along about 1903, the one-cylinder, two-cycle, make-and-break engine came into existence. It gained rapid popular acceptance. Cats designed solely for sail were converted to power, and new cats were designed to be fitted with power. By and large, the conversion to cat power took less than a decade. However, even after power had proved its worth, old-timers remained suspicious of it. A cousin of my father had a cat, the *Bunny,* that was equipped with a brand new engine. *Bunny* wasn't rigged up, but she did have a mast and some idea of a sail that my father's cousin always carried along because he didn't trust the engine. The amazing thing was that, for all his distrust, he never had any trouble with that engine. Other fellows who knew more than he did about engines used to have trouble now and again. But he never did. It seemed as if the good Lord was with him.

THE ONE-LUNGER

For several decades, the original one-cylinder, two-cycle, make-and-break engine was standard for a catboat auxiliary. They were colloquially known as "putt-putts" and "one-lungers." The two preferred makes among catboat people were Lathrop and Palmer, although other manufacturers also produced them.

Few engines can equal a one-lunger for simplicity and economy. Our old single-cylinder Lathrop engine could virtually run under water. That is to say, with the engine hatch off and the spray going all over, the engine would run and never miss a beat. The only thing that might stop it would be a solid water bath in the mouth of the carburetor. Lately, the one-lunger has undergone a revival. A currently available model is the Acadia engine made in Nova Scotia.

When *Vanity* was built in 1929, my father put in a Lathrop six-horse, one-cylinder, two-cycle engine. It had a five- or six-inch bore with a 5½-inch stroke, and it had tremendous torque. It swung an 18 x 24 propeller. The 18 stands for inches of diameter. The 24 stands for inches of pitch. If a propeller were to travel through a solid block of space, in one turn around, measured at the widest section midway of the blade, it would travel 24 inches or two feet. Even after allowing for slippage, an 18 x 24 propeller moves a great deal of water in each revolution, which is another way of saying it can push a boat forward or backward.

There was also available in the old days a two-cylinder, two-cycle engine, but not many catboat owners used them. These were equipped with a reversing gear, while the one-lunger had direct drive and no reverse gear. Instead, the one-lunger reversed "on the switch." The ignition switch could be turned off at a strategic point in the cycle. If switched on again at the right moment, the engine

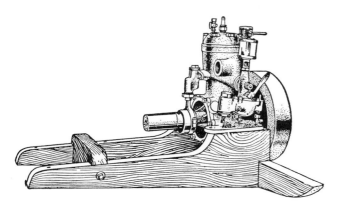 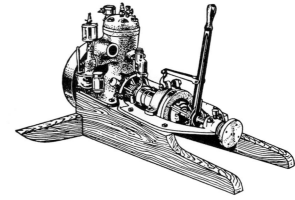

A typical one-lunger mounted on an engine bed. This is a Ferro Special, shown without a reverse gear on the left and with one on the right. Most *catboats dispensed with the gear and reversed "on the switch." (Peter H. Spectre Collection)*

reversed itself. Some fellows used to get the same effect by holding the flipper, the outside part of the make-and-break mechanism. The flipper was fixed to a shaft that went through the head to the ignition points inside. If a piece of scallop twine were tied to the flipper and held tight, one could feel when it came, made, and broke. About the last of the revolution if you let go, the engine wouldn't fire. Consequently, there wouldn't be enough power to bring her clear over when the cycle came around again to compression. It would catch just as it got to the center. Then when the engine fired it would go back the other way in reverse. Ordinarily you could stop within a boat's length with a string reverse, but if you had headway and nothing happened when you pulled the string, you were in trouble. Many a time, a boat would run into the stern of another boat or hit the dock because the reverse didn't work.

The putt-putt was fairly high measured from crankcase to cylinder top. In this respect, it was somewhat like some of the small diesels that are around today. Its height made for an awkward and cluttered cockpit. When *Vanity* had her first six-horsepower engine, we had a box in the cockpit that towered above the cockpit floor.

THE FOUR-CYLINDER, FOUR-CYCLE ENGINE

In 1938 we got an LH 4 to replace our Lathrop putt-putt. This was a four-cylinder, four-cycle engine. Its cylinders were half the size of those on the one-lunger. It was both more efficient and more

complicated than the putt-putt. It turned up a higher RPM and produced greater horsepower. It would also allow greater speed. This is not too important in a catboat, whose very hull shape limits its speed, but nevertheless, the four-cylinder, four-cycle engine gradually replaced the one-lunger. The fact that my father had a putt-putt as late as 1938, however, indicates how successful the early make-and-break engine was.

In the LH 4, the H stood for Hercules, because Lathrop was then using a Hercules industrial engine block with a marine conversion. Of course, the LH 4's came equipped with a reverse gear, so some of the fun of reversing "on the switch" or by pulling on a piece of scallop twine disappeared forever. The 1939 LH 4 was rated 38 horsepower at 2,800 RPM. In 1957, I installed a new LH 4. It is rated at 45 horsepower. Also, in 1937, Lathrop offered a small flywheel as optional equipment. Today there is only one flywheel size available. But in 1937 you could get either a small 12″ flywheel or a large 18″ flywheel. My father decided upon the small flywheel, because it would give him more depth between the bottom of the flywheel and the water that would gather in the bilge. Built as a party fishing boat, *Vanity* is equipped with a well, and the well is just ahead of the flywheel, so that two or three buckets of water in the engine room would practically fill her up to the flywheel.

Our LH 4 swings a 16 x 10 propeller, and this is considered big for the size of the engine because she will not turn up to the RPM of her rated horsepower. We have direct drive and don't use a re-

Pamir IV, *a German-built catboat, uses an unusual single-cylinder horizontal diesel engine. This 10 horsepower engine of German manufacture is only 15 inches high, enabling it to be installed under a flush cockpit deck.*

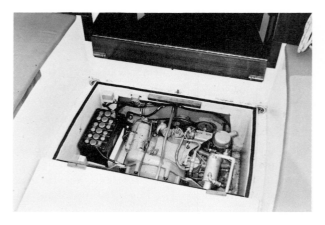

duction gear. Such gears are generally used to turn a bigger propeller at a slower RPM. Phil Norton once had a la'nch with a 30 horsepower Grey equipped with a reduction gear that he used for towing. The gear gave a 2½ or 3 to 1 ratio with an 18 x 10 propeller. As a result, the la'nch had tremendous power at the touch of her throttle.

Today there is quite a wide variety of small power plants suitable for inboard power in catboats. Among them are the Universal Atomic 4, the Universal Bluejacket Twin, the single-cylinder Palmer of about eight horsepower, and the larger 24-horsepower four-cylinder Palmer. There is also available a small one-cylinder, two-cycle Acadia engine. In diesel engines there is the small Lister, the Volvo Penta, and several others.

OUTBOARD ENGINES

Many of the smaller cats, including the Marshall 18, the Hermann cat, and almost all the half-decked daysailers are too small for inboard power. Peter McCormick made a study of outboards back in 1967 when he owned a Marshall Sanderling. What he found was that the outboards for this purpose should have a long shaft and a reversing gear. Since not much power is needed to drive a small fiberglass or wood cat, he narrowed his choice down to engines in the five- to ten-horsepower range. Weight becomes a consideration, because these engines hang on a bracket mounted on the transom or in some cases on the rudder. Consequently, horsing them in or out becomes a real operation. The alternative is to leave them on the bracket and buck them up so they clear the water. However, this is unsightly and the weight astern affects the balance of the boat. A six-horsepower engine is about as heavy an engine as can conveniently be placed on and off the rear bracket. The length of shaft is important in two respects. A short bracket mounted outboard may on occasion bite the rud-

Engine	Power	Cyl.	Prop.	Dry Weight	Approx. price 1967
Evinrude Fisherman 6 Johnson Compact 6 (same) with long shaft, clutch and fwd/neut/rev.	6 at 4500 RPM	2	2 blade 8 x 7¼	51 lbs.	$296.50
Evinrude Angler 5 Johnson Compact 5 (same) with long shaft but no fwd/ neut/rev.	5 at 4000 RPM	2	3 blade 8 x 7½	43 lbs.	$246.50
British Seagull Century Plus with clutch and long shaft.	5 at 4000 RPM	1	5 blade 11″ dia.	37 lbs.	$210.00

Most of the long shaft models are five inches longer than the standard shafts but the Evinrude Angler 5 is available as well with an "extra-long shaft," 15″ longer than the standard.

der. This, however, can be controlled by installing a stop. More important, the long shaft gets the propeller down in solid water, where it has less of a tendency to cavitate and actually gives greater driving force.

Peter found that the choice, taking all these factors into consideration, boiled down to three basic options among five engines then available.

Probably the specifications for these engines have changed since Peter made his study, but the basic ideas for an outboard suited to a catboat are pretty much the same today as they were then.

SHAFT HOLES AND SHAFT LOGS

Catboats that were built for sail alone had solid deadwood aft. When power became available, some boatbuilders drilled with an auger from outside the deadwood up through the keel to provide for the propeller shaft. Other builders ran the shaft outside the keel, putting what they called a cheek block up against the deadwood. The cheek block can best be imagined by considering a lead pencil split longitudinally. One half would be the cheek block while the lead would be the shaft. The cheek block was screwed up tight against the deadwood and cut off flush with the end of the deadwood. The stuffing box was set in the after end with its bolts in both the deadwood and the cheek block. Of course, with this arrangement, the engine was not in the center of the keel but was mounted off to one side a little bit.

For new boats, a shaft log was developed to fit within the keel and the deadwood. I recall watching Manuel Swartz Roberts construct a shaft log. He first cut the main part of the keel to a certain angle. I don't know how he assumed this angle, but apparently he had an idea in the back of his head as to how it should be. He made the shaft log in two pieces by cutting out the center on a circular saw to a depth of one half the width where the shaft was going. After grooving, he would remove whatever excess wood there was with a chisel. Then he would put the two pieces together with the joint horizontal and bolt them in place. After fitting the shaft log, Manuel continued the keel above the shaft log to get whatever depth he wanted for the deadwood. He put stopwaters in the joints of the deadwood and shaft log at the extreme after end of the keel to check possible leaks. As its name implies, the stopwater actually stops water from getting into the shaft log at the joint. It is made by drilling a small hole, ½″ or less, right through the deadwood at a corner of the joint where the shaft log begins and the seam of

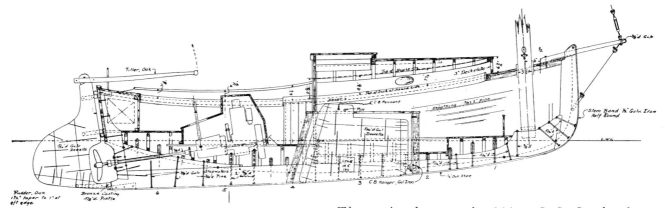

The engine box on the 16-foot S. S. Crocker-designed cat Dog Watch *takes up the lion's share of the cockpit.* (The Rudder *magazine*)

the deadwood backside rise or stern post joins the shaft log. The hole is plugged with a round dowel that swells in place, keeping the water out.

The shaft log should be caulked along the joint. Otherwise it can leak at this point. This is a particularly vulnerable spot on a cat that has dried out, because the shaft log will tend to open up. However, the fact that the shaft log needs recaulking is easy to overlook because the deadwood appears to be too solid to let water get into the hull no matter how dried out it becomes.

FUEL SYSTEMS

In the early days when gasoline engines were first installed, the gas tanks were built into the quarter behind the staving. Some cats had tanks on both quarters. The tanks used to be gravity feed and, for the most part, the engine carburetor would be lower than the tank was. In later years, the tanks were put up forward next to the cabin. Some working catboats that weren't used for partying even had tanks inside the cabin. They'd be set on stilts in a way that would make it possible to have gravity feed. In later years, in an effort to get weight low down in the hull, some owners of catboats used as yachts had the tanks installed under the cockpit floor. Naturally, it was necessary to use a fuel pump to get the gasoline into the engine because the tanks were set too low for gravity feed. Nevertheless, the feed line installed below the cockpit floor in this manner was, at first, run out of the bottom of the tank. Nowadays, the feed line comes out of the top of the tank. This top-feed arrangement constitutes a problem for tanks with gravity

feed, because if the gas gets low in the tank the suction can be broken. Then suction has to be restored by disconnecting the gasoline line and sucking on it to get suction going again. Danny Gaines once installed a rubber squeeze bulb in the gas line to get suction restored when the gas ran low. On the few times that he lost suction, he reached down and squeezed the bulb and she started right up again.

With a gravity-feed line that comes out of the bottom of the tank, you are more apt to get sludge and dirt than from a gravity-feed line that comes out of the top of the tank. However, with feed from the top, you have to have cushion gas in the tank that you can never use. Danny Gaines has a 20-gallon gravity-feed tank with a feed line coming out of the top of the tank, but he can't use the last five gallons in the tank the way it is hooked up. Location of the fuel shut-off valve on a gravity-feed line can sometimes cause trouble if it is brought up too high in relation to the bottom of the tank and the height of the carburetor.

All gasoline lines should be equipped with filters. The heavy bronze marine model is the proper kind. However, I have an automobile-type filter with a glass bulb on *Vanity*. Filters should have a petcock in the bottom to drain off water that might accumulate without bothering to take the thing apart.

LAYING UP — FULL TANK VS EMPTY TANK

I think myself that on laying up a boat, all gasoline should be taken out of a tank because, after four months, gasoline starts to go stale. I have known gas to be left in a copper tank over a winter to become like jelly by spring. The tank and lines had to be removed and washed out with alcohol to get them free.

In theory, a full tank checks condensation of moisture. But I can't see where you can get any condensation to speak of out of a dry tank. I doubt very much if an empty tank is any more of a fire hazard than a full tank. If the gasoline fill cap is left open, the fumes can escape if the tank is really dried out with care. Some tanks are hard to drain completely because they have a filler neck that goes down to the bottom. If the tank is absolutely level, it's a hard thing to get the tank absolutely empty by suction. If the tank is on a slant and has a drain at a low point, of course, there is no problem.

GUM IN GAS

There is a certain amount of gum in gasoline to begin with. You can detect it by sniffing. Gas that has gum smells sort of rank and doesn't have that true, fresh, gasoline smell. Gum causes trouble, because the gas gets on to the valve stems when the engine is run and warms up. Then when the engine is shut off, the gum in the gas congeals on the valve guides and causes sticky valves. Commercial solvents such as "Liquid Wrench" or "Mystery Oil" when squirted into the cylinders through the sparkplug holes will free up the valves. But it is very hard to detect sticky valves as a cause of engine malfunction and even harder to detect gum in gasoline as the cause of trouble. If an engine won't run and you find yourself saying, "It ran OK the day before, why doesn't it run now?", it's likely that gum is making the valves stick, particularly if this happens at the beginning of the season. There is a commercial product called "Gum Out" that I have found is very good for getting rid of gum in gasoline. Put in the gas tank, it also cleans the inside of the carburetor where you can't get at it and it does get at sticky valves.

"Dry Gas" is another good product. According to claims on the can, it does almost the same thing as "Gum Out," but it also converts condensed moisture in the gas into a burnable substance. Getting rid of condensation is its main virtue.

LAYING UP AN ENGINE

What should one do on laying up an engine? The instructions on lawnmower engines and such tell you that if the engine is to be laid up more

Chat Frais, *later* Semper Fi, *a 21-foot Herbert F. Crosby and Sons cat of 1929, bowling along under power. (William Dillon)*

than 30 days, the gas should be drained from the carburetor and the tank. If it is to be laid up six months or more, the sparkplugs should be removed and a tablespoon of oil put in each cylinder. The engine should be turned over by hand to distribute the oil throughout the pistons and around the valves. The battery should be removed and put in a warm cellar at home and preferably put on a trickle charger so it doesn't run down.

It is important on laying up an engine to provide for its cooling system. Most catboat engines are cooled by salt water. Frequently, a by-pass is provided in the water line. This is a good thing because it keeps the engine above 140° and at a proper operating temperature that stops condensation in the base. My first LH 4 was torn down when she was 10 years old to put in new rings. All the carbon and sludge in the base could be put in a teaspoon. If the coolant water had been circulated just as it came in from the sea, she undoubtedly would have had a lot of sludge in the base. Salt water forms in crystals if the engine gets too warm. It forms in hot spots in the engine where water isn't circulating as it should. Air is what causes corrosion and helps scale to form. With mine, when I'd take the head off, I'd shake the head to get out the scale and I'd flush the water jackets out with fresh water. Nowadays, in laying up an engine, a permanent type anti-freeze should be put in the engine to protect the cylinder walls. The anti-freeze has rust inhibitors in it that give added protection to saltwater-cooled engines. To get the anti-freeze in the engine, the inlet hose is pulled off and the engine is started out of water. The anti-freeze mix is in a five-gallon container, and the inlet hose is dipped in the container so that the anti-freeze is pumped through the engine. When the colored anti-freeze mixture starts coming out of the exhaust, the engine is shut off. The hose is either pulled off and plugged or pulled up high enough so that gravity will keep the anti-freeze in the engine head and thus left there all winter long. In the spring, the salt water lines are worked up and the anti-freeze is kicked out to sea.

It is well to check the valves in an engine at lay-up time. My valves didn't need doing for four years. Yet, when the valves were getting near the point that they did need grinding, I could tell in cold weather when I'd crank the engine. In "barring her over with a crank" (some of the very early engines were cranked with a long bar that fitted into slots in the flywheel, hence the colloquial expression), you can feel the compression you get on each cylinder. So when you bar over and find one cylinder doesn't have the compression of the others, there is reason to be suspicious. Sometimes when the engine is firing on all four cylinders, you can hear that the explosions aren't even and one cylinder may sound weak. That, too, indicates that you need a valve job.

COMMISSIONING AN ENGINE IN THE SPRING

In the spring, new plugs and wiring harness might solve ignition problems, but it probably isn't necessary to replace them unless the engine has been run a lot. Of course, most yards, as a general thing, do replace plugs and points as a business proposition. In any case, the ignition wiring, plugs, and harness, should be checked and, if necessary, replaced.

Multiple-strand insulated copper wire will often be corroded by action of the salt and become ineffective without showing outward signs of weakness. The low-tension wire is of this kind and sometimes causes trouble. It should be checked or replaced. This winter I had a novel kind of trouble that had its roots in a defective low-tension wire. I turn off my engine every time I end my drift in scalloping and then start her up when I'm ready to drag again. I had some bother with my starting switch when I'd push it all the way in to start the engine. Sometimes it wouldn't contact, but when I'd take my finger off the button it would contact. I put a new switch on and tried that but it wouldn't always contact either, so I brought home the wire that went from the switch to the ground and tested it with 110 volts. It seemed OK but the switch still wouldn't contact. I finally put a new wire in and that cured the problem. The multiple-strand wire had corroded to the point that it was unreliable, although it still looked good.

Chapter 13

A CATBOAT BIBLIOGRAPHY
by John M. Leavens

Notwithstanding its great popularity, there is no single definitive book on the catboat. In its heyday, the catboat was so common that it was taken for granted. Even the major builders didn't bother to maintain adequate records of the cats they built.

Generally, catboats, unless used commercially, weren't big enough to require official registration with an appropriate agency of the United States government (in general, the U. S. Customs Service) as were large vessels, although some were so registered from 1867 to the World War I era. From World War I until enactment of the Motor Boat Act of 1938, all powerboats, including auxiliaries, were required to be officially registered. References are made hereinafter to the series of annual volumes of *Merchant Vessels of the United States* listing vessels officially registered.

With the enactment of the Motor Boat Act of 1938, and until the early 1960's, jurisdiction (including licensing authority) over motorboats not officially registered was vested in the U. S. Coast Guard. Since the early 1960's, the licensing of powerboats not officially registered has been vested in agencies of the respective states. So far as is known, neither the Coast Guard nor the respective state licensing authorities have published listings, annual or otherwise, of licensed boats, although it is sometimes possible to trace an individual catboat if the license number is known.

Various yacht registers, dating from 1872 on, do list catboats, but it is sometimes difficult to separate cats from other listed craft.

The literature of the catboat is both sporadic and thin. Here and there a chapter dealing with catboats is found in a book on small craft. Often the material is erroneous, or copied from other sources, or both.

Much catboat history and background can be found in early magazine articles. A dedicated catboat historian can also dig up much original catboat material in local histories or ancient issues of newspapers published in areas where catboats were built and sailed.

Articles on catboats can be found in such publications as *The Skipper, Yachting, The Rudder, National Fisherman* (and its predecessor, *Maine Coast Fisherman*), *Soundings, Classic Boat Monthly*, and occasionally other magazines. Included herein are selected articles on catboats from such publications but the list is not all-inclusive.

BOOKS (*indicates out of print)
American Sailing Craft by Howard I. Chapelle, 1936, Kennedy Bros. Inc., New York. Chapter 4, "The Cape Cod Catboat," is similar to the material in the article, "The Cape Cod Catboat" in Volume 52 of Yachting, page 53, November, 1932 by the same author. It is an account of the Crosbys of Osterville, Massachusetts, illustrated with lines drawings of four Crosby cats. Two are Horace S. Crosby models of 1870 and 1883 and two are H. Manley Crosby models of 1895.

American Small Sailing Craft by Howard I. Chapelle, 1951, W. W. Norton & Company, Inc., New York. In Chapter 5, "Sloops and Catboats," Chapelle discusses, among other things, the Newport boat, the Providence River boat, the waterboats, the New York sloop (fitted with an alternate mast hole forward for ready conversion to cat rig) and the Eastern or Martha's Vineyard catboat.

The Boy, Me and The Cat — Cruise of the Mascot, 1912-1913 by Henry M. Plummer, 1914, New Bedford, Massachusetts. Original edition written, illustrated, typed, mimeographed, and bound individually by Henry M. Plummer. Reprinted in book form, 1961, the Cyrus Chandler Company, Rye, New Hampshire. This delightful and classic account of a father-and-son cruise on the 24'6" catboat *Mascot* from New Bedford to Miami, Florida and return is "must" reading for all catboat buffs.

The Cape Cod Catboat by David B. Crosby, 1958, typescript of a paper submitted in a course of Techniques of Educational Research (institution unknown). In this paper, reference is made to the "Private Journal of Manley Crosby," no trace of which has come to light. The latter journal is credited with the anecdote of the catboat *Mblem*, built by H. Manley Crosby, being caught in such a severe storm that, allegedly, the varnish was washed off her cabin house.

Captain Nat Herreshoff by L.Francis Herreshoff, 1953, Sheridan House, New York, is the biography of Captain Nathanael G. Herreshoff, the author's father. It contains many references to catboats, including a list (possibly incomplete) of Herreshoff-built catboats. It also mentions *Julia*, a 23-foot cat-rigged keel Point-style boat built in 1833 by Charles Frederick Herreshoff.

The Cat Book — Containing the Designs and Plans of Twelve Cat-Rigged Yachts (Reprinted from The Rudder), 1903, Rudder Publishing Co., New York. Mostly the cats shown are turn-of-the-century racing cats. Lines drawings, plans, and sail plans are given for each of the 12 designs. Because many of the builders are unknown today and the designs range from 1873 to 1896, the book is an interesting historical record. Among the designers, T. E. Ferris, Mortimer H. Smith, A. B. Babbit, V. D. Bacon, H. C. Wintringham, and A. Cary Smith were well-known marine architects of the time whose catboat designs probably were casual and incidental to their main designing work. But Thomas R. Webber, Wilton and H. Manley Cros-

by, and C. C. Hanley were renowned for their catboats *Camilla, Scat, Step Lively*, and *Harbinger;* all household names in their day. The list of all 12 designs follows:

T. E. Ferris — "15 foot keel catboat," 22'8 x 15'0 x 7'8, 1896.
Mortimer H. Smith — *Hilda*, 18'6 x 9'10, 1896.
A. B. Babbit — *Varuna*, 20'5 x 10'0, 1891.
Thomas R. Webber[1] — *Kittie*, 27'0 x 9', 1894.
Wilton Crosby — *Scat*, 25'11 x 10'0, 1896.
V. D. Bacon — "Twenty One Foot Racing Boat Designed For *The Rudder*," 30'0 x 21'3 x 10'2, not dated.

H. C. Wintringham — *Uarda*, 30'0 x 11'0, 1896.
Mortimer H. Smith — *Swananoa*, 30'0 x 11'5, 1896.
H. Manley Crosby — *Step Lively*, 34'6 x 11'2, 1896.
A. Cary Smith — "Twenty-Five-Foot Boat," 33' 0 x 25'0 x 11'4, designed in 1896 "for use in Florida waters."
T. R. Webber — *Camilla*,[2] 27'5 x 12'6, 1873.
C. C. Hanley[3] — *Harbinger*, 28'0 x 13'6, 1889, "twenty-eight foot cabin boat successfully raced for several seasons in Eastern waters."

The Compleat Cruiser by L. Francis Herreshoff, 1956, Sheridan House, New York. This fictional story of the catboat *Piscator* and the ketch *Viator* cruising in Cape Cod, Nantucket, Martha's Vineyard, and Rhode Island waters weaves in the origins of various cat-rigged craft, including the Woods Hole spritsail-rigged boat, the periauger or West Island boats (a double-ender cat ketch), and the early Newport "Point" boats. In addition, the author suggests Rhode Island as the birthplace of the catboat.

The Cruiser. From 1906 on, Rudder Publishing Company published a series of annual volumes of sea stories under the name *The Cruiser*. Many of the stories in these annual volumes deal with catboats. The exact number of annual volumes issued is uncertain, but probably there were not more than 10, if that many.

[1]of New Rochelle, New York.
[2]Camilla's lines are those of a classic plumb-stem, plumb-stern catboat. Her half model is now in the Mystic Seaport collection.
[3]of Monument Neck, in what is now Buzzards Bay, Mass.

Cruising Boats Within Your Budget by John Jacob Benjamin, 1957, Harper Brothers, New York. Chapter 2 contains a brief apocryphal account, reported factually, of how the cat got its name, e.g., "comes about quick as a cat."

Fore and Aft — The Story of the Fore and Aft Rig by E. Keble Chatterton, 1912, J. B. Lippincott Company, Philadelphia, and Seeley, Service & Co., Ltd., London. This book has a page on the "cat-boat type of craft" accompanied by an illustration of an "American Cat-Boat — the mast is stepped very far forward as in the Dutch-American sloops of the seventeenth century." Chatterton, a well-regarded English author, also claims, "In this cat-boat type of craft we have a clear descendent of the Dutch influence, with no jib, but the mast stepped right in the eyes of the boat." He also says, " . . . historically she is related to the Norfolk wherry . . ."

Fore and Afters by B. B. Crowinshield, 1940, Houghton Mifflin Company, Boston. This book has but a half page and two pictures (*Iris* and *Elvira*) on catboats.

The Fore-and-Aft Rig in America by E. P. Morris, 1927, New Haven, Yale University Press; reprinted in 1970 by Library Editions, New York, N. Y. Chapter 4 is entitled, "One Masted Rigs: The Dory. The Catboat." Morris notes: "In 1870 catboats were very common about New Haven, many of them by no means new, and it is safe to say that type and name go back to 1850 and probably to 1825."

Fore and Aft Sailing Craft and The Development of the Modern Yacht by Douglas Phillips-Birt, 1962, Seeley, Service & Co., Limited, London. In less than a page, and using the catboat illustration from Chatterton's book, Phillips-Birt agrees with Chatterton about the cat rig being "a throw back to the old Dutch rig . . . and . . . the Norfolk wherry . . . " He does, however, refer to the catboat as "another type no less characteristically American."

Gaff Rig by John Leather, 1970, International Marine Publishing Company, Camden, Maine. This book contains an excellent chapter on catboats.

A History of the Westhampton Yacht Squadron 1890-1905 by Standish F. Medina, 1965, privately printed by the Westhampton Yacht Squadron Ltd.,

Westhampton, Long Island, New York. This book has chapters on "Sailboat Racing, Pre-1890," the "Sandbag and Slide Rule Era of the East Bay Cat-boat — 1890 to 1910," and the "BB Catboats — 1901-1908." East Bay is, of course, on the south shore of Long Island. The BB catboat was a 25' decked racing cat created by the Great South Bay master builder, Gil Smith.

Joy's Pier by Philip N. Case, 1951, Dorrance & Company. Recollections of a boyhood spent at Oak Bluffs on Martha's Vineyard where party cats and their hardy owners flourished from 1903 to World War I.

Little Cruises of the Onkahye by Winfield M. Thompson, c. 1908, Rudder Publishing Co., New York. Tales of cruises in New England waters in a catboat told by a master story-teller. (See also references to Thompson's articles on catboats in early issues of *The Rudder*, under *Magazines and Periodicals*.)

The Middle Road by Llewellyn Howland, 1961, The Concordia Co., Inc., South Dartmouth, Massachusetts. Includes the tale of the catboat *Bruiser*, winner of the Battle of Priest's Cove.

The National Watercraft Collection by Howard I. Chapelle, United States National Museum — Bulletin 219, Washington, D. C., Smithsonian Institution, 1960. Contains references to catboats and cat-rigged boats, including a description and picture of a model of a cat-rigged Gloucester water-boat, complete with rigging. There are also brief descriptions of the "Eastern Catboat 1875-80" and the "Providence or Newport Boat." References are also made to the "Florida Cat-rigged Sharpie Oyster Boat" and the "Biloxi Catboat." Unfortunately, none of the described cat-rigged boats are illustrated.

The Rudder Treasury — Edited by Tom Davin, 1960, Sheridan House, New York, includes the following reprints of articles from back issues of *Rudder*:

Solitude, a cat yawl, 20' — Murray G. Peterson (June 1890).
Sea Hound, A Crosby Cat, 25' — Charles Crosby (April, 1912).
A 24' Keel Catboat — Winthrop L. Warner (April, 1951).

Sailing Craft by Edwin J. Schoettle, 1928, the MacMillan Company, New York, reprinted 1955. A number of articles in this sailing anthology deal with catboats. Among them are:

> *American Catboats* by Edwin J. Schoettle, in which the author contends that catboats "were in use at an earlier date on Barnegat Bay, New Jersey than on any of the more easterly bodies of water."
>
> *The Toms River Cup* by Commodore Edward Crabbe describes catboat races at Toms River, New Jersey, in the 1870's.
>
> *Taft Cup Catboats* by F. G. Luderer deals with the special variety of racing catboat developed to compete on the Great Lakes in 1911 for a cup given by President William H. Taft (hence the name) and still going strong.
>
> *Barnegat Bay Sneak Boxes* by O. G. Dale, and *Fifteen Foot Sneak Boxes and Junior Sailing on Barnegat Bay* by Charles E. Lucke, Jr. These two articles trace the development of the cat-rigged Barnegat Bay gunning boat and the cat-rigged pleasure and racing craft which derive from it.
>
> *The Atlantic City Catboats* by William Wood and Bennet C. McNulty. This article describes the small, decked, low-headed cat dating around 1913 and sailed in the inland waters behind Atlantic City, New Jersey.

Sailing Craft at Mystic Seaport by Edouard A. Stackpole and James Kleinschmidt, 1960, Marine Historical Society, Mystic, Connecticut. This pamphlet, now out of print, has a brief section on catboats, with pictures.

Small Yachts — Their Design and Construction Exemplified by the Ruling Types of Modern Practice, by C. P. Kunhardt, 1887, Forest & Stream Publishing Co., New York. Contains two sections, one on centerboard catboats and one on keel catboats. The section on centerboard catboats has four parts:

> *A Portable Cat* (10 feet overall).
>
> *A Newport Cat* — The 20-foot "Newport catboat is of the local variety uncolored by the late invasion of Narragansett waters by ideas from the outer world of Yachting." The illustration of this catboat portrays a keel that is absolutely flat with no trace of rocker.
>
> *An Eastern Catboat* — The catboat portrayed is similar to those in the well-known Currier and Ives lithograph "Blue Fishing." Kunhardt

says of this 15'6 cat that it has "the lines of a boat hailing from Duxbury."

> *Rigs of Eastern Centerboard Catboats* — This table lists centerboard cats ranging from 11'3 lwl (5'3 beam) to 25'1 lwl (11'6 beam). The section on keel catboats has three parts:
>
> *The Caprice* — A 20-foot keel cat built by Woods Brothers of East Boston in 1881 "for service between Boston and Marblehead and in adjacent waters."
>
> *The Dodge No. 2* — An 11'11 lwl craft, the prototype of which was built in England as a tender to a schooner yacht.
>
> *Rigs of Keel Catboats* — The table on rigs of keel cats ranges from 10'8 lwl (4'10 beam) to 21' lwl (9' beam).

Sou'West and By West of Cape Cod by Llewellyn Howland, 1948, Harvard University Press. Delightful tales of a New England upbringing that included sailing on Buzzards Bay in an 18-foot decked spritsail-rigged boat.

Traditions and Memories of American Yachting by W. P. Stephens, 1942, reprinted from *Motor Boating* by Hearst Magazines, Inc., New York. The second edition published after 1942 includes three additional sections, Parts 37, 38, and 39 titled "East of the Cape," which offer interesting, albeit somewhat disjointed, reminiscences of catboats. Stephens was the first librarian of the New York Yacht Club, and his book is a treasure-house of information on early yachting.

Wherries and Waterways by Robert Malster, 1971, Terrence Dalton Limited, Lavenham, Suffolk, England. The story of the cat-rigged Norfolk and Suffolk wherry, which is a "first-cousin, once removed" of the American catboat.

Yankees Under Sail edited by Richard Heckman, 1968, Yankee, Inc., Dublin, New Hampshire. This book contains the reprint from Yankee Magazine for June, 1965, of John M. Leavens' illustrated article: "Nine Lives of a Yankee Catboat," a good capsule story of the origin and uses of the catboat.

MAGAZINES AND PERIODICALS

The yachting magazine evolved relatively recently, say 1890 or thereabouts. Before that day, there were yachting or boating sections to outdoors-type magazines such as *Forest and Stream* or *Outing*, but even such magazines seldom go back as far as the early 1870's. Occasionally, too, an article on yachts appears in a magazine of general interest such as *The Century* or *Harper's New Monthly Magazine*. For all practical purposes, only a few magazines with good material on catboats are most likely to be accessible to students of catboat history today. What follows is a list of key articles.

*The Catboat Association Bulletin — Volumes 1-39, October, 1961 - November 1, 1972. Includes a great deal of material on catboats, their origin, development, and usage. This is, perhaps, the best single concentrated source of information on the catboat. Because of their collective importance to catboats both generally and specifically, a classified outline of some of the major articles to be found in the *Bulletin* follows:

	Bulletin	Date	Page
Catboat Association, The			
Organization Concepts	# 1	(9-20-62)	1
A word about . . .	2	(2- 1-63)	2
Catboat Register	2	(2- 1-63)	2
Burgee, specifications	12	(6- 1-65)	4
Burgee, colors	12	(6- 1-65)	Cover
John Killam Murphy Award	13	(10- 1-65)	1
Committee on Future	14	(1- 1-66)	1
Authorized	30	(3-15-70)	3
Proposes Changes	32	(10-15-70)	1
Report of	33	(3-15-71)	Sup. 3
Steering Committee			
Authorized	33	(3-15-71)	3
Builders and Designers			
Anderson, Charles, 1871-1953, of Wareham, Mass.			
More about Anderson Cats	5	(10-28-63)	10
Note	11	(5- 1-65)	3
Crosby of Osterville, A Note on			
by John M. Leavens	3	(5- 8-63)	Sup.
Carter, Frank			
Carter South Bay Cat	26	(4- 1-69)	10
Hanley, C. C., Monument Beach and			
Quincy, Mass.			
Forgotten Master of Shoal Draft			
Design, by John M. Leavens			
1. The Days at Monument Beach	29	(1- 1-70)	Sup. 1
2. The Shop at Quincy Point	30	(3-15-70)	Sup. 1
3. The Yard at Germantown	31	(6- 1-70)	Sup. 1
4. Last Years	32	(10-15-70)	Sup. 1
Comments by Fenwick C. Williams	33	(3-15-71)	15
Thordis	29	(1- 1-70)	Cover
Phinney, William W. 1865-1946, Monument			

The Rudder. Early issues of *The Rudder* contain considerable material on catboats, including lines, photos, and brief squibs about boats and races. The catboat articles of two authors, Thomas Fleming Day and Winfield M. Thompson, are particularly outstanding.

"The Catboat" (in 3 parts) by Thomas Fleming Day, appeared in September, 1896, October, 1896, and January, 1897. Day discourses on the distinction between "cat" and "cat-rig" and offers believable comments on the origins and evolution of the catboat.

"Where The Cape Cats Breed" by Thomas Fleming Day, published in 1902 (Volume 13, page 981) is a description of Osterville and the Crosby shops at the turn of the century.

"A Catboat Sailor's Yarn" (in two parts) by Winfield M. Thompson, April and May, 1906, is a delightful, rollicking tale of *Twister*, a 28-foot cat built by Daniel Crosby.

"Sea Wolf, Cruising Cat" by Winfield M. Thompson, 1909 (Volume 21, page 124 — precise date unknown) tells the story of a big Crosby cat.

"Cats in Massachusetts Bay" (in two parts) by Winfield M. Thompson, January and February, 1908, tells of catboat racing on Massachusetts Bay in 1907.

"The Second Interbay Catboat Match" by Winfield M. Thompson, October, 1910, is the story of the competition among catboats from Massachusetts Bay, Narragansett Bay, and Barnegat Bay in the summer of 1910.

"I Buy an Old Cat" by Winfield M. Thompson, 1911 (Volume 25, page 299 — precise date unknown) is the story of *Duster*, a C. C. Hanlet cat of 1892 vintage.

"Why I Chose a Catboat" by Daniel B. Streeter.

"Sea Hound, A Real Catboat" (Volume 27, page 290, 1912) describes the 25-foot Charles Crosby catboat that is still winning catboat races today.

There are other articles and lines drawings of catboats in issues of *The Rudder,* far too numerous for detailed listings.

Yachting. Over the years, stories on catboats have appeared in the pages of *Yachting* magazine, of which only a representative sample is listed below:

    1912, Volume 28 (page 276) "New Taft Cup Catboat"

    1914, Volume 30, "The Cat That Came Back" by Winfield M. Thompson

    November, 1932, "The Cape Cod Catboat" by Howard I. Chapelle

    April, 1944, "In Defense of the Cat" by William B. Oehrle

    July, 1953, "In Praise of the Cat" by J. S. Pitkin

    March, 1954, "The Biography of a Catboat" by Charles H. Vilas

    December, 1964, "The Other Man's Boat" by Charles W. Wittholz and Alex Mitchell describes the catboat *Prudence.*

    March, 1965, "The Cat With More Than Nine Lives" by Irwin Anthony records class A catboat racing on Barnegat Bay.

    March, 1966, "Gilbert (Gil) M. Smith, A Great South Bay Legend" by W. H. (Ham) deFontaine, Paul Bigelow collaborating.

    February, 1969, "The Return of the Catboat" by Daniel B. Streeter.

    July, 1971, "The Toms River Challenge Cup" by Bill Robinson.

Other magazines which may contain early material on catboats are:

National Fisherman/Maine Coast Fisherman
    June, 1964, "My Search for the *Big Nickerson*" by John M. Leavens, reprinted from the Vineyard Gazette for May 1, 1964.

    July, 1965, *"Cygnet Dan"* by John M. Leavens.

    February, 1965, "Catboat Buff Details Hours of Work That Lie Behind Quality Wood Craft" by J. Whit Anderson; the story of *Lobelia.*

    September, 1969, "Fat Cats Were The Do-All Boats When Island Fishing Had Its Day" by John M. Leavens.

Cape Cod Compass, 1964 Annual, "The Cape Cod Catboat" by John M. Leavens.

Long Island Forum, June 1966, July 1966, "Gil South, Master Boat Builder" by Paul Bigelow.

The Log (of Mystic Seaport), Fall, 1971. ". . . Quick as a Cat!" by John M. Leavens.

American Neptune (quarterly)
Fore and Aft
Sail and Sweep
The Yachting and Boating Monthly
Motor Boating
The New England Yachtsman (monthly, 1937-1941)

In addition, W. P. Stephens in *Traditions and Memories of American Yachting,* Part 22, lists a number of early periodicals that included articles on contemporary yachting.

The Aquatic Monthly and Nautical Review — "devoted to the interests of the Yachting and Rowing Community," first published in June, 1872.

Brentano's Monthly — "that treats of yachting among 21 sporting interests." It was first published in 1873.

Forest and Stream — first published August 14, 1873, and, for many years, a leading yachting periodical.

The Country — a sports weekly that took up the subject of yachting around 1878.

The Spirit of the Times — "a weekly chronicle of the Turf, Field, Sports, Agriculture, and the Stage" (c 1872). It frequently carried gossip and news of yachting.

A CAT ALBUM

Nok-Nok. *Maud E. Backus owned this curious little catboat being sailed in West Bay, Osterville, by "Con-Con" Driscoll in 1897. She is heading for the boat shop of Herbert F. Crosby. (Osterville Historical Society)*

Victor. *Long a Vineyard Haven party boat,* Victor, *26' x 12' 9", was built by Wilton Crosby in 1916. Foster Nostrand, a half owner at the time, snapped her off Fort Totten, New York, in the early 1960's. The shot shows how her halliards are led aft to the* cockpit *and cleats on the bulkhead for ease in handling. It also shows emergency steering lines, attached to the horse or traveller, running back to an eye hole at the outer end of the barn-door rudder. (Foster C. Nostrand)*

Hawk. *Bowling along on a close reach past a barrel day marker, Hawk, pedigree unknown, is apparently off on a cruise with three aboard. Someone has done a neat job of coiling the anchor rope on the cabin house roof. (Nathaniel L. Stebbins / Society for the Preservation of New England Antiquities)*

Pet. *Somewhere in New England around 1900, this rugged, open-cockpit, half-decked daysailer must have provided many interesting hours of sailing in a harbor crowded with shipping. Judging from the length of boom projecting beyond the clew and the single row of reef points, Pet must have carried more sail at one time. (Nathaniel L. Stebbins / Society for the Preservation of New England Antiquities)*

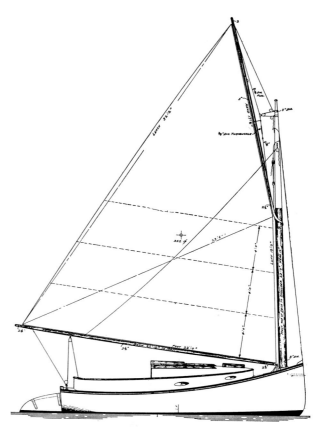

Cumbrae, *21' x 10' x 2' 6", designed in 1932 by Fenwick C. Williams, provides cruising features usually found only in boats over 30'. Cumbrae was actually built in 1947 by Hubert Johnson of Bay Head, New Jersey, for Dr. Edward Pyle of Waterbury, Connecticut. She was subsequently owned by the late Dr. A. Whitney Griswold, one-time president of Yale University in whose honor she wears a distinctive Yale-blue sail. She is now owned by Leland S. Brown of Chappaquiddick Island, Martha's Vineyard, chairman of the Steering Committee of the Catboat Association.*

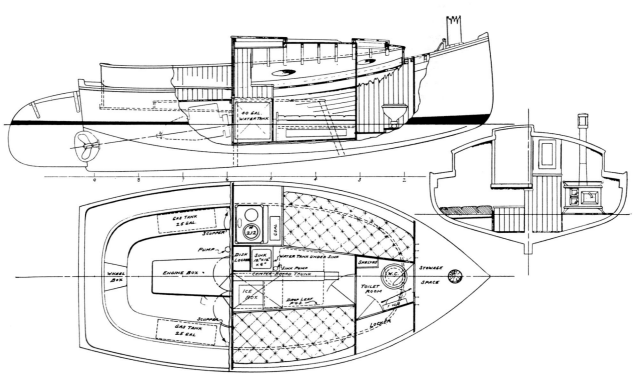

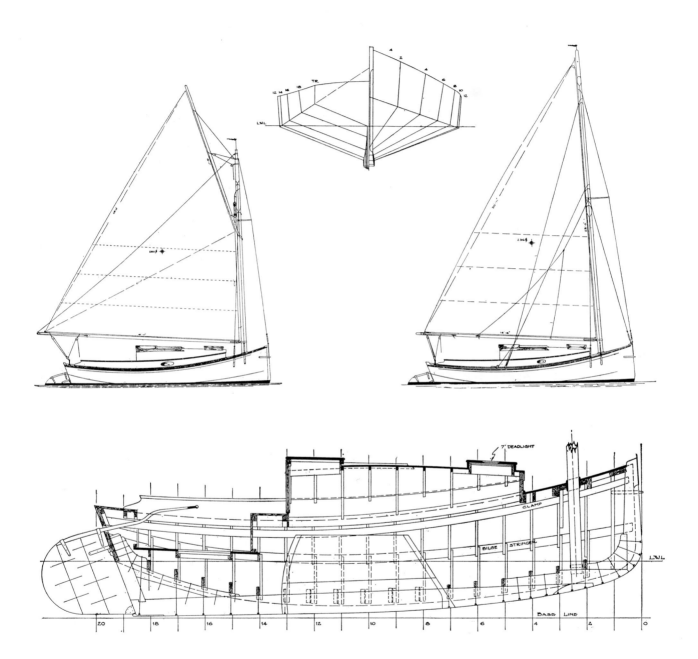

F. A. Dugan designed this vee-bottomed cruising cat. It is said to have been "not expensive to build, easy to handle alone, with sufficient weatherliness for coastwise work and with comfortable accommodations for two." Notwithstanding her dimensions of 20' x 15' 1½" x 8' 7" x 2' 1", she features a small toilet room forward, with a dresser and clothes locker set off from the rest of the cabin by a bulkhead just forward of the centerboard trunk. Gaff and marconi rigs were provided as alternatives, with moderate sail areas of 260 and 236 square feet respectively. (The Rudder magazine)

Myth. *This roomy cat with a huge three-port cabin and large mainsail is apparently being single-handed with ease in Boston harbor. There are no clues to her builder, but the step up as her coaming cap rail approaches the cabin house is apt to be found in Massachusetts mainland cats, such as those of Briggs of Westport and Pierce Brothers of Boston. (Nathaniel L. Stebbins / Society for the Preservation of New England Antiquities)*

Tang *reefing. Reefing, while under way, can be difficult when it breezes up.* Tang *is rolling and pitching on Long Island Sound, and she doesn't seem to want to come up into the wind. It would* have helped if the sheet had been lashed down tighter before reefing began. (Boothman Marine Photography / Saybrook Studio)

Imp. *Edson B. Schock designed* Imp — *14' 3" x 6' 9" with 157 square feet of sail area — for Thomas Fleming Day, editor of* The Rudder. *Her lines were published in the July, 1907, issue as* Sea Wren, *and she was built in 1911 by Church of Wyandotte, Michigan. Edson B. Schock was the first of three successive generations of designers of catboats in the same family. (David E. Woehler, Jr., present owner of* Imp)

Prudence. *(Douglas Photo Shop / Roy Blaney)*

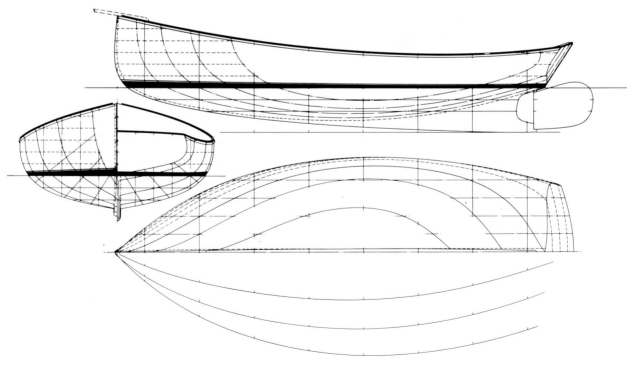

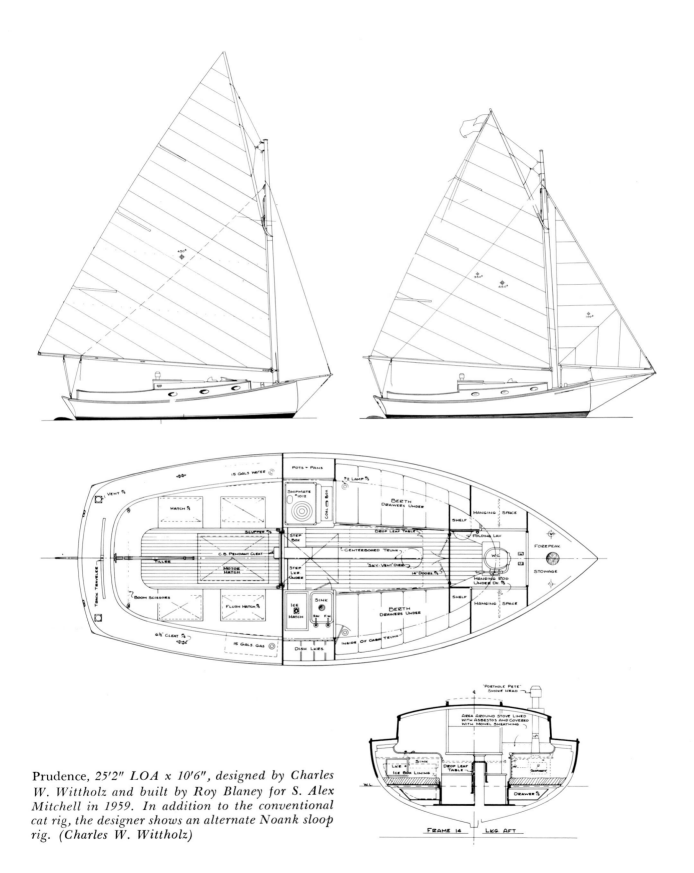

Prudence, *25'2" LOA x 10'6", designed by Charles W. Wittholz and built by Roy Blaney for S. Alex Mitchell in 1959. In addition to the conventional cat rig, the designer shows an alternate Noank sloop rig. (Charles W. Wittholz)*

The Old Sculpin. Manuel Swartz Robert's boat-shop in Edgartown in the late spring of 1946 is the setting for the "l'anching" of the 22-foot cat Roberts built for William Nerney of Oak Bluffs. The shop was named The Old Sculpin after columnist Joseph Chase Allen's affectionate nickname for Roberts. The boat, too, was so named. (Clair Birch)

Volante. *Power comes in handy in a dead flat calm.* Volante *tows* Rosebud *and two other cats home at Nantucket around 1915. (Charles F. Sayle)*

Patchy Fog. *Fenwick C. Williams designed this 18-foot cat for the John G. Alden Office. She was built in 1955 by Story. Originally* Marsh Nymph, *then* Wicked Queen, *and now* Patchy Fog, *she is driving* *to victory in the July, 1971, Paule Stetson Loring Trophy Race on Narragansett Bay, with every one of her 264 square feet of sail area working for her.* (Providence Sunday *Journal / Cyril H. Buckley)*

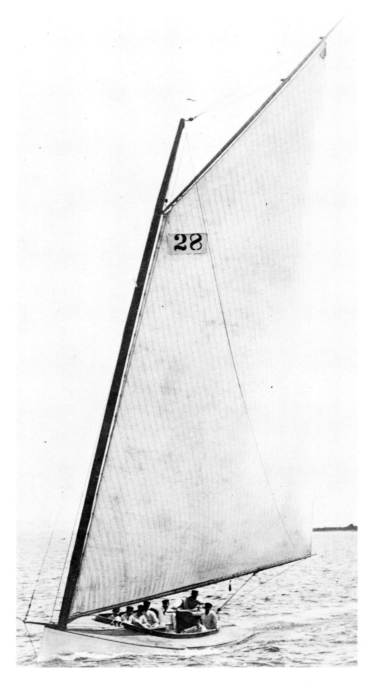

Tattler's *lines, sharp plumb stem, large cockpit, tall mast, huge sail, eight-man crew, and tiller steering all say sandbagger. J. S. Johnston, a New York photographer took this shot in 1891. (Collection of John M. Leavens)*

Crosby gathering in 1888. Among those in this September 1888 shot in front of the Worthington Crosby (1823-1898) shop at Osterville are: Front row (left to right): James Leonard, Warren Lovell, Worthington Crosby, Oliver Coffin. Rear row (left to right) Charles Lewis, Ralph Crosby, H. Manley Crosby, Harold Crosby, Joseph Crosby, two unidentified boys standing behind Joseph Crosby, Billy Granger, Wilbur Crosby, Alexander Bacon and Charles Hall. (Osterville Historical Society)

Daniel Crosby, 1850-1920, a famous Osterville, Massachusetts, builder of catboats, posed in 1880 for this picture. (Osterville Historical Society)

Two cats, Calynda *on the East Coast and* **Sharon L** *on the West Coast, resulted from this design by Fenwick C. Williams for the John G. Alden office in 1931. As cats go, this is a design of generous proportions. Her dimensions are 28′ x 12′ 6″ x 3′ 2″ with board up. "Below she has sleeping accommodations for four persons with two berths up forward, hanging shelves and a hatch up through the forward end of the trunk cabin for fresh air. The main compartment has a berth on the starboard side with a hinged upper berth over it and a good sized hanging locker just inside the companionway. To port there is a lavatory, a seat, and a small coal stove. The ice box is under the flooring on the starboard side and the coal box is in the corresponding space to port. A drop leaf table is, of course, arranged on the centerboard trunk. . . "* *One has to live aboard this boat to appreciate the spaciousness of its accommodations.* Calynda, *now owned by Arthur and Rosalind Northrop of Mattapoisett, Massachusetts, has been changed to cat yawl rig.* Sharon L, *owned by Miles and Louellen McCoy of Orcas Island, Washington, retains the cat rig, but with a small jib set on a short bowsprit for ease in handling.* (The Rudder *magazine)*

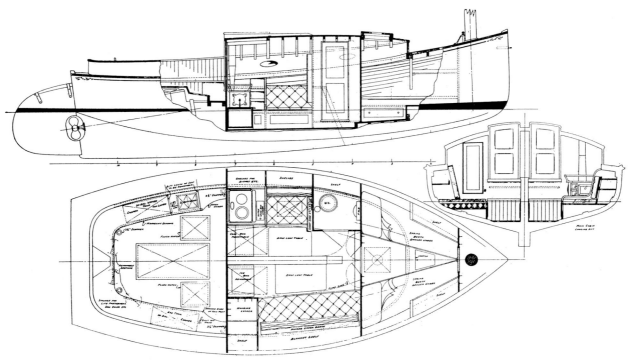

114

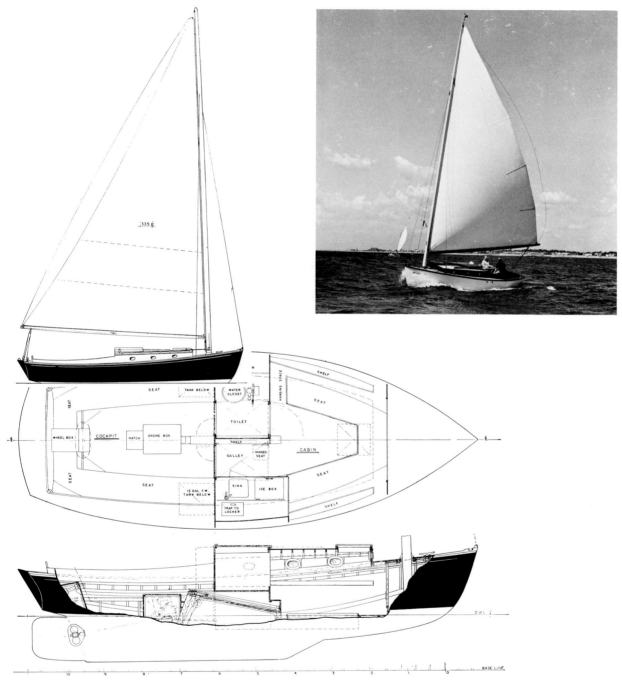

Compromise *is the only known cat to have been designed by Sparkman and Stephens. She was built in 1951 by Freeport Point Shipyard, Freeport, New York. For more than a decade she has cruised out of Northport, New York, with Dr. Mary E. Bradford and an all-girl crew. Her dimensions: 23' 11½" x 19' 9½" x 9' 10" x 2' 6", represent a compromise with classic catboat lines, hence her name. She is a bit narrower and has slightly longer overhangs than is customary. Her 335 square feet of marconi-rigged sail befit her slightly rounded stem and counter stern. Her double companion is flanked by a separate enclosed head on one side and a convenient galley on the other. (Saybrook Studio /* The Rudder *magazine, August 1952)*

Nantucket ambience. Her mast and sail mirrored in still waters, a catboat drifts idly in this turn-of-the-century period piece. (Edouard A. Stackpole collection)

Virginia. This open-cockpit Great South Bay racing cat, caught coming about in 1935, has typical G. L. Smith features: low flat sheer, counter stern, long after deck, tiller steering, long oval cockpit, and gently curving stem. Her mast is steeved slightly forward. Aloft she has a double bridle for her peak halliard and spreaders to improve the effectiveness of her shrouds and forestay. (Robert Snyder)

Tartar. *This plumb-stem, plumb-stern cat with the tall spar, large sail, tiller steering, and five-man crew is a sandbagger of the mid-1880's. Her lap-* *strake hull is unusual in a cat-rigged boat. (Nathaniel L. Stebbins / Society for the Preservation of New England Antiquities)*

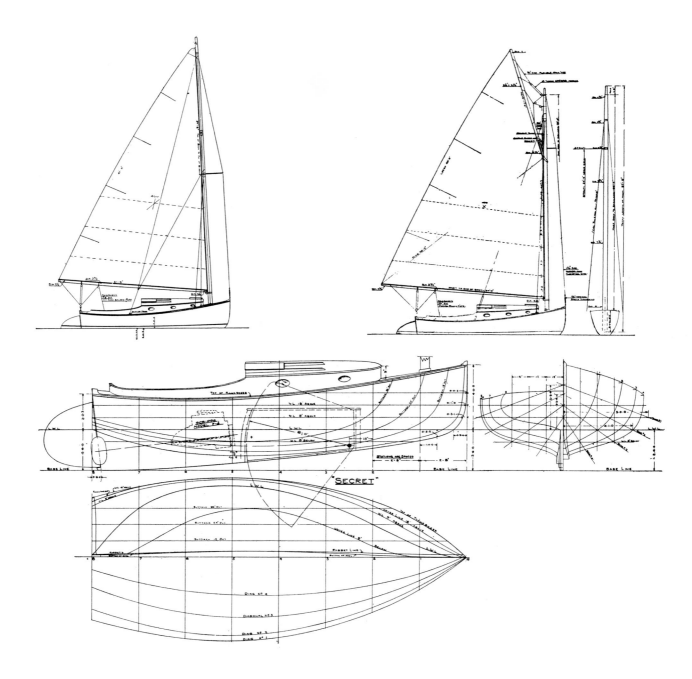

"SECRET"

Secret, *designed by Francis Sweisguth and now owned by L. Huntington Brown of Mt. Kisco, New York, is one of three sister cats, the others being* Manx *owned by Robert F. Dunlap of West Islip, Long Island, New York, and* Lady Lou V *owned by John D. Beinert of Babylon, New York.* Secret *was the prototype of the full-scale fiberglass Americat 22 production series built in 1972 by George Benedict of Sayville, Long Island.* Secret *and her sisters were built in the years 1927-1930. They have proven to be exceptionally fast and able. The original design provided for alternative gaff and marconi rigs. Dimensions are: 22' x 21' x 9' 9" x 2' 6". The relatively tall rig and above average sail area (490 square feet in the gaff rig version, 400 square feet, marconi) coupled with below average beam, account, in good part, for the fine turn of speed in* Secret. (The Rudder *magazine, December 1931)*

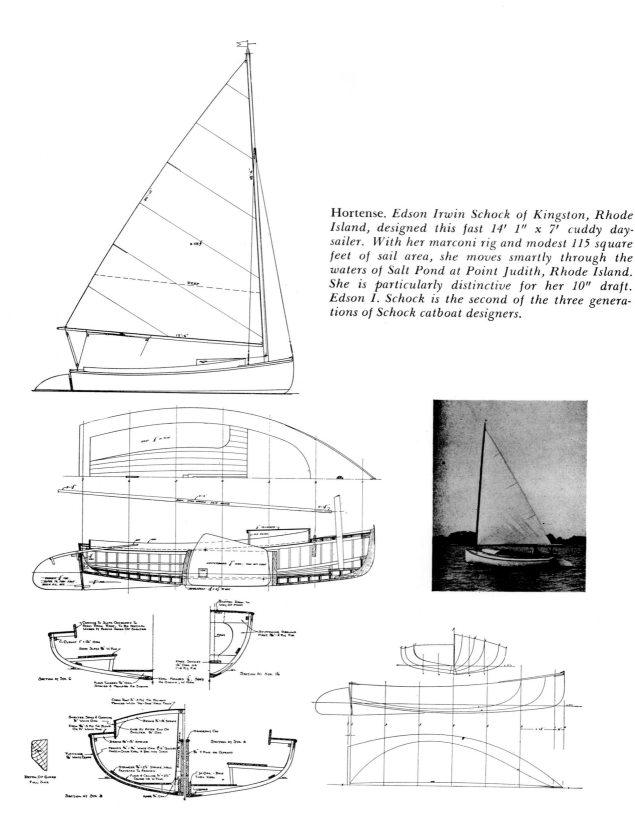

Hortense. *Edson Irwin Schock of Kingston, Rhode Island, designed this fast 14' 1" x 7' cuddy day-sailer. With her marconi rig and modest 115 square feet of sail area, she moves smartly through the waters of Salt Pond at Point Judith, Rhode Island. She is particularly distinctive for her 10" draft. Edson I. Schock is the second of the three generations of Schock catboat designers.*

Kiowa *sails gracefully somewhere, sometime in the 1890's. While she appears to be a huge, half-decked, open-cockpit cat, actually there is a large houseless cabin forward. (Nathaniel L. Stebbins / Society for the Preservation of New England Antiquities)*

Dot. *Great South Bay could be the home of this fantail-stern cat of the 1890's, for she is fitted with a "sun" or "summer" cabin featuring a fixed roof and roll-down canvas curtains. (Collection of John M. Leavens)*

Wilton Crosby's work crew in 1900. Standing in front of Wilton Crosby's shop, as identified by Malcom (Uncle Max) Crosby in 1964, are (left to right): Henry P. Leonard, "a young fellow just starting in," Azor or Asa Hall, a carpenter "who got out the planing of the wood for the boats," Ro-

land Ames, "one of Uncle Bill's finest carpenters and joiner men," Stephen (Steve) Bates, a painter, Warren Lovell, another painter, George Williams, carpenter, and Wilton Crosby himself. (Osterville Historical Society)

Dartwell. *High jinks aloft on* Dartwell, *a famous racer built by C. C. Hanley in 1895. (Wayne Blake Collection)*

Idler. *Not much is known about this heavily canvassed cat of the 1890's-1900's, but she carries a boom of tremendous length, which shows why cats of this type quite often had to be reefed. Legend has it that such a reef was shaken out by a man walking along the boom when the breeze died out.*

It is unusual to find a cat of this size with tiller steering. Given the known weather-helm characteristic of the cat, it must have called for more than one man on the helm on many an occasion. (Nathaniel B. Stebbins / Society for the Preservation of New England Antiquities)

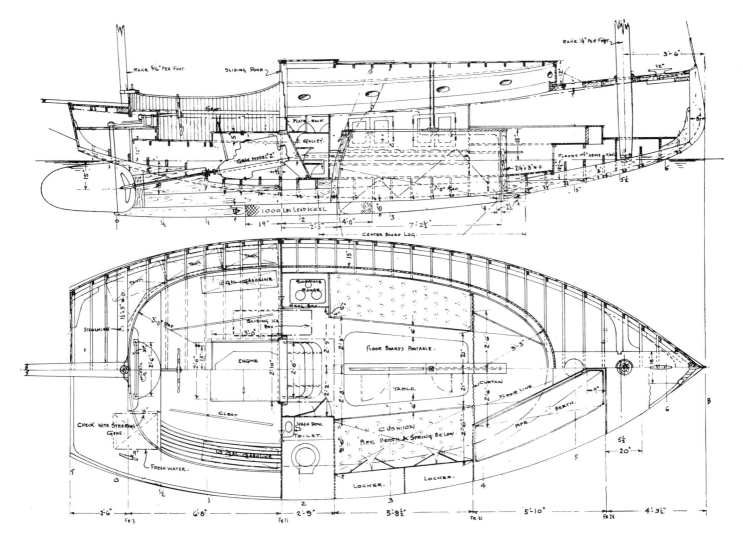

Two Sisters, *now* Mollie B *and owned by Paul and Mollie Birdsall, co-secretary and treasurer, respectively, of the Catboat Association, is the only cat yawl to have been designed by C. C. Hanley. She was the last boat he designed. She was built in 1927 by the Baker Yacht Basin at Quincy, Massachusetts. Erland D. Debes of Wollaston, Massachusetts, collaborated in the design.*

This cat yawl "gives great roominess for its length, shallow draft for tidal waters, handiness about floats, and general handiness. The double rig was chosen in order to keep the main boom entirely inboard, to save reefing, and because of the undoubted value of the spanker when lying at anchor in keeping the boat head to the wind. The

gaff rig was preferred to a jib-header as a means of getting good sail area without tall spars and a multiplicity of rigging. The principal dimensions of Two Sisters *are as follows: LOA 27' 9", LWL 24', beam 11' 9", draft, without board 2' 6", draft, board down 6' 9". A 4-cylinder Gray motor drives her close to 8 miles an hour..."*

On March 14, 1971, Mollie B *narrowly escaped destruction in a spectacular $2,000,000 fire that destroyed the Essex (Connecticut) Marine Railway yard. Although declared a total loss by the insurance company, she was sold back to Paul Birdsall and he has succeeded in restoring her completely. (Saybrook Studio / Yachting magazine)*

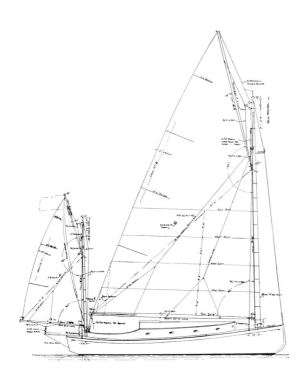

Ebb Tide. *John Dexter of Mattapoisett built* Ebb Tide *in 1926. She was 22' 10" x 10' x 2'10". Her boom rests in a scissor-type crutch.*

Running cat. The skipper of this fast-moving, decked cat is too intent on the photographer to notice how his bellying sail has lifted his boom dangerously, but the result is a charming shot of a catboat running before the wind.

Honey Boy. *The elaborate guying system for* Honey Boy's *marconi mast indicates the serious problems involved in supporting a tall stick in the eyes of a catboat where the width at the deckline is too narrow for effective results. (The Peabody Museum of Salem)*

Hustler. *Action is the word as the racing cats go downwind with jibs wung-out. Hustler, in the foreground, is a former Chatham fishing cat built by one of the Crosbys and later part of the fleet that raced in the 1908 events of the Quincy (Mass.) Yacht Club. (Nathaniel L. Stebbins / Charles W. Wittholz)*

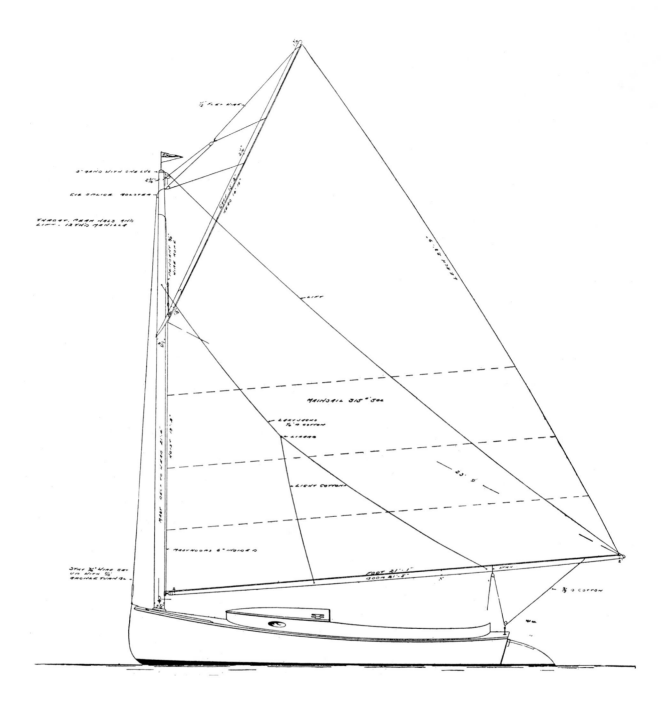

A catboat daysailer with cuddy cabin designed by W. H. Hand, Jr. Her over-all length is 17.58 feet; her waterline length is 16.33 feet. She has a beam of 7.75 feet, a draft of 1.81 feet with the board up, and 1,000 pounds of inside ballast. She carries 315 square feet of sail.

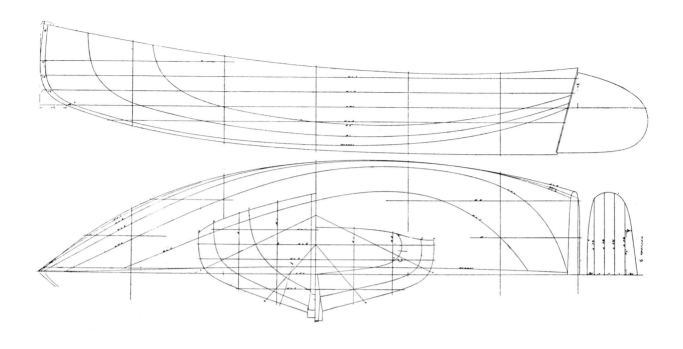

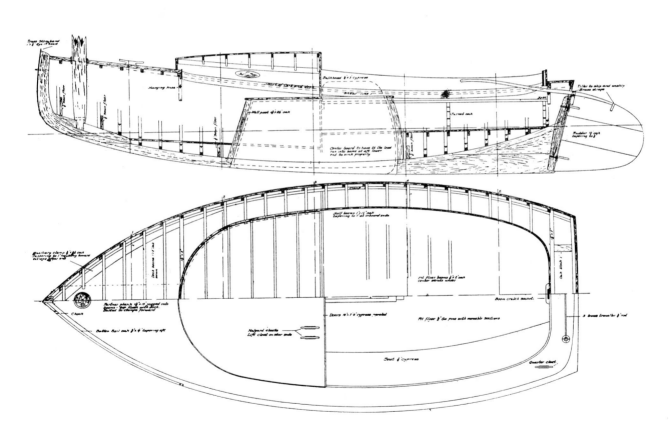

129

Lance. *This elegant 40-foot cat yawl with her somewhat clipper bow was built at Fall River by Reed Brothers for Andrew Borden in the early 1890's. (Nathaniel L. Stebbins | Society for the Preservation of New England Antiquities)*

Ruth. *Fenwick C. Williams writes: "The old* Ruth *with overhang stern that I photographed at Marblehead was used as a party boat in Gloucester for many years. She was 24 feet LOA and was said to have belonged to Grover Cleveland, as was said of all cats named* Ruth. *Maybe they all did. She was a nice appearing 24 footer, built by Crosby, I feel certain, with that very fine feeling for line and form which seemed to be shown in the best examples."* Ruth *has the short-cabin, long-cockpit characteristic of fishing party catboats. (Fenwick C. Williams)*

Susie. *Except for her jib and long bowsprit, Susie, with her gently curving stem, appears to be a large, comfortable, cruising cat of perhaps 28 feet or so. Her "up and down" sail is fitted with four rows of grommets for lace-line reefing. (Nathaniel L. Stebbins / Society for the Preservation of New England Antiquities)*

T. E. Ferris designed this 15-foot keel cat in 1896. The term "15" refers to waterline length. Her other dimensions were 22' 8" x 15' 0" x 7' 8". Keel cats are uncommon. They tend to be sluggish in coming about and sacrifice many of the advantages of the shoal draft centerboard cat. (The Cat Book, 1903, Rudder Publishing Co., New York)

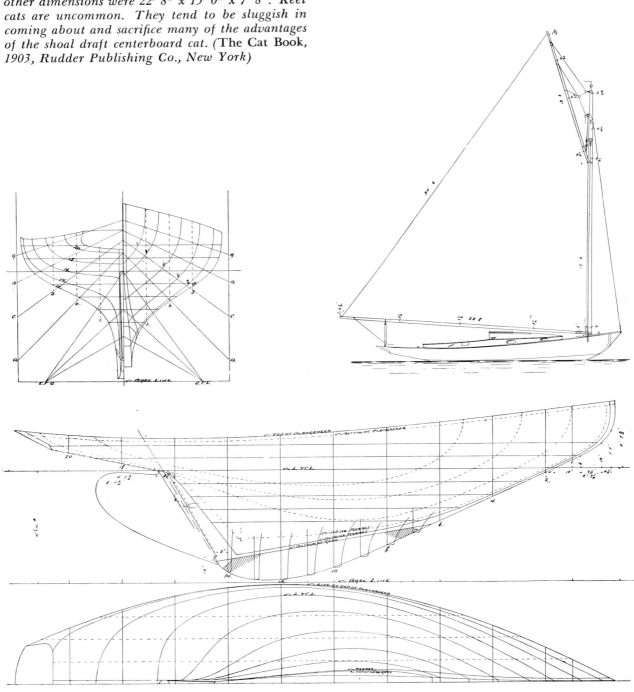

V. D. Bacon's "Twenty one foot racing boat designed for The Rudder," *not dated, is 30' 0" x 21' 3" x 10' 2" x 1' 7". The design follows a passing turn-of-the-century trend toward long overhangs for catboats. Extremes of this sort led the Interbay Catboat Association in 1910 to condemn "freak features" in catboats. (*The Cat Book, *1903, Rudder Publishing Co., New York)*

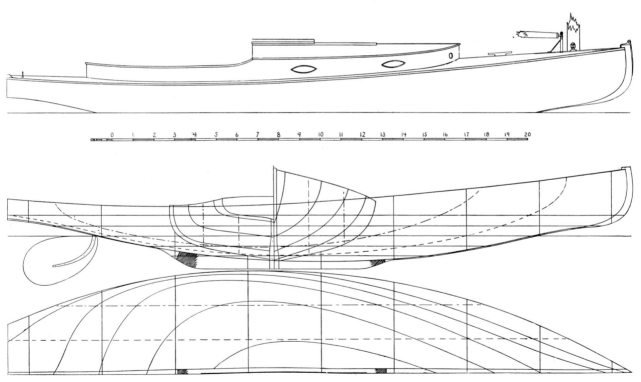

Mayflower. *W. W. Phinney, 1865-1946, built the 30-foot keel cat* Mayflower *at Monument Beach, Massachusetts, in 1909. She spent many years at Woods Hole as a workboat for the A. C. Harrison family. She was originally named* Passer-by, *a name which attests to Harrison's sense of humor and his knowledge of the performance of a big keel cat. This photo was taken in July, 1965, at Oyster Bay, Long Island. She is shown being sailed by Henry M. Kidder, her then owner, the third such in 56 years. (John M. Leavens)*

Charles H. Crosby, 1854-1936, photographed in the early 1930's. He went into partnership with his father, C. Worthington Crosby, and his brother Daniel in 1872. Worthington retired in 1890, but Charles and Daniel continued together until 1901 when Daniel set up a new firm with his son Ralph. Charles continued to build independently until the early 1930's. Sea Hound, *built in 1911, is an outstanding example of his craftsmanship. (Osterville Historical Society)*

Thordis, *shown in 1902 flying a huge jib from a long, hogged bowsprit. Thordis was C. C. Hanley's catboat masterpiece. She was built at Monument Beach, Massachusetts, in the winter of 1896-97 for Thomas B. Wales of Wellesley Hills who had a summer home on Buzzard's Bay. She measured 33' 4" x 23' 11" x 11' 3" x 2'. Her least freeboard was a scant 1' 10". In the summer of 1897, Thordis won 17 races out of 17 starts. Her great success and very* shallow hull is perhaps responsible for the epithet "skimming dishes" that became current at the turn of the century. Her model became one of Hanley's two basic designs, serving as the prototype for sloops up to 65 feet in length. Now rigged as a cat yawl and owned by Jack Maselli, Thordis *still sails in New York waters. (Nathaniel L. Stebbins / Foster Collection)*

Fred W. Goeller, Jr. was well known in the first decades of the twentieth century for his catboat designs. This 1912 design for a 22' 5" x 11' 0" x 2' 3" cat illustrates the difference in catboat sail area before power and after power. The descriptive text, written in 1912, notes that: "The sail plan was kept small to obviate the necessity for reefing when the breeze freshens up a bit." Yet the sail plan provides for 539 square feet of sail area and four sets of reef points. Comparable sail area for a cat of this size after power would be 350 to 425 square feet, with two, or at most three, sets of reef points. One commendable feature of the step-down cabin is the separate hanging locker to starboard. (The Rudder magazine, Volume 28 [1912])

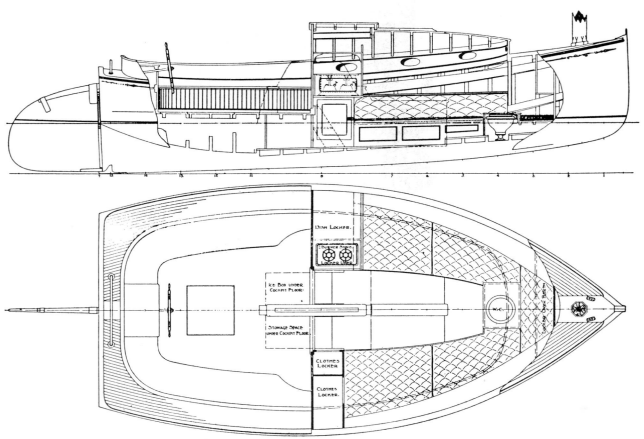

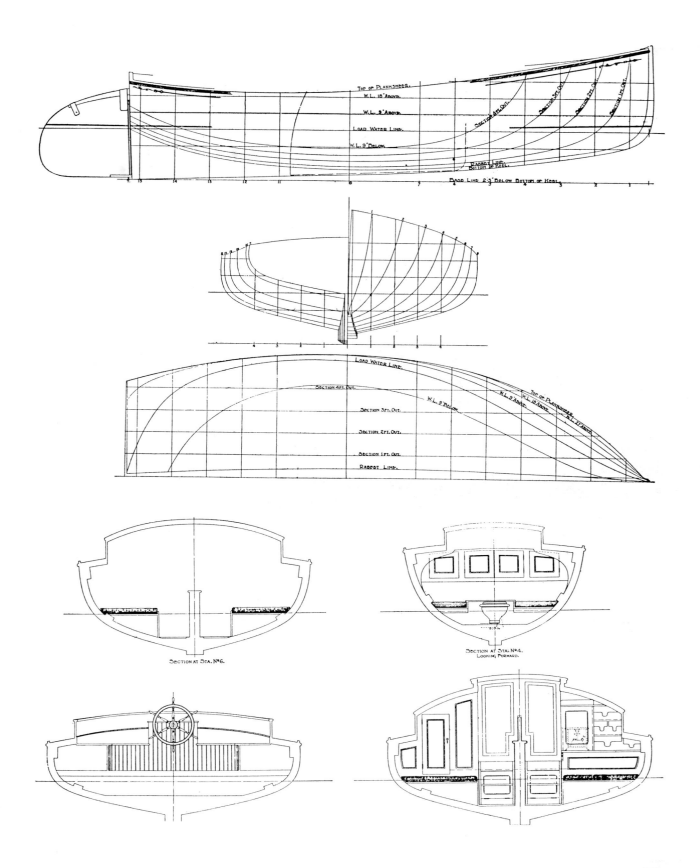

Samoset, *33' x 13' 6", with two reefs in, drives through breaking seas off Nantucket's Coatue Beach in this dramatic shot made in 1900 by a photographer identified only as H. M. C.*

Cleopatra. *Famous for her stars and stripes sail, Cleopatra lies at the end of old North Wharf, Nantucket, in the 1880's. Her transom is decorated with lotus leaves and other Egyptian ornamentation* *befitting a Cleopatra. This 37-foot cat was owned by A. O. Russell of Cincinnati, Ohio, and skippered by Captain George W. Burgess of Nantucket. (Charles F. Sayle)*

138

Mary. *They don't come much prettier than Mary, a big, comfortable cat, with a whopping cabin, complete with forward hatch and center skylight. Mary's gaff and luff are attached with slides rather than jaws and hoops. No. 59 to the right is a sandbagger type. Time is the 1880's. (Roger C. Taylor)*

Sea Hound, *built by Charles Crosby of Osterville, Massachusetts, in 1911 for Charles H. Lord of New Haven, Connecticut, is 25' 9" x 25' x 11' 6" x 2' 8". Originally she had 725 square feet of sail area. She was one of four cats all built at Osterville about the same time and based around New Haven that had similar names:* Sea Mew, Sea Horse, Sea Wolf, *and* Sea Hound. *They constituted the mythical "sea-class" of catboats.* Sea Hound, *now owned by Dr. Robert C. Ascher of New York, was extensively rebuilt for family cruising in the early 1960's. She is a "true Cape cat in every respect": square, broad stern, and underbody kept well down with a barn-door rudder found on most cats in Cape Cod waters. While a very full-bodied boat, her lines are all long and easy, giving wonderful qualities of seaworthiness, speed, and room. Her racing qualities have been amply demonstrated in recent years. Despite her more than 60 years of age, she has often beaten the more buoyant, smooth, fiberglass cats on a boat-for-boat basis. (Collection of John Killam Murphy/* The Rudder *magazine)*

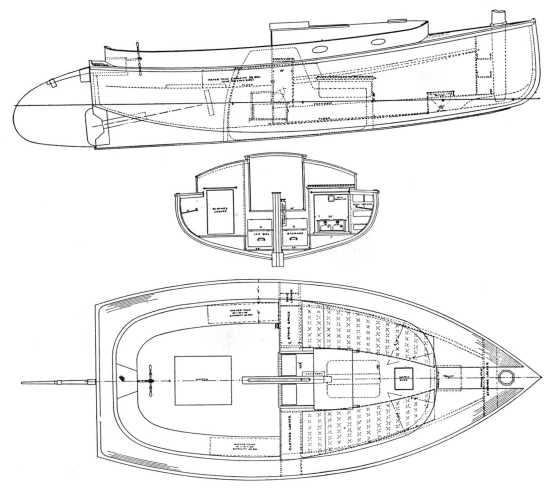

Nantucket's Steamboat Wharf around 1900. The cat at the left is unidentified. Eleanor *and* Lucille *are at the right.* Eleanor's *outboard rudder is of a type that antedated the barn-door variety. (Charles F. Sayle)*

Ulula. *Stebbins caught* Ulula *skirting a "stern and rockbound coast," but left no clues to its identity. The time is in the 1890's. (Nathaniel L. Stebbins / Society for the Preservation of New England Antiquities)*

Cleopatra *was built by C. C. Hanley some time before 1896, and possibly as early as 1892, for Melbourne MacDowell, the actor, husband and manager of Fanny Davenport, the actress.* Cleopatra *was named for the tragedy in which Fanny played the lead. This 21-foot half-decked cat was the first known Hanley model to depart from classic Cape cat lines, for she was built with long overhangs fore and aft. Her cross-cut sail sports five sets of reef points.* Cleopatra *was fast. She is said to have won eight straight against all comers. Picture taken in 1896. (Nathaniel L. Stebbins / Foster Collection, Hart Nautical Museum, Massachusetts Institute of Technology)*

142

Catboat raft. Some 14 cats raft in Hamburg Cove on the Connecticut River on August 17, 1963, following the Essex Yacht Club's Marston Trophy Race. (John M. Leavens)

Herbert F. Crosby, Sr., 1853-1936. Herbert F. Crosby began building boats at Osterville in 1880 with three of his brothers, but he broke away and set up his own shop at the foot of Bay Avenue in 1882 where he continued to build actively for 50 years. His last boat was the catboat Charlotte II, *now* Pinkletink. *This picture taken in the 1930's shows him at the end of his career. (Osterville Historical Society)*

Iris. *Herreshoff Manufacturing Co. of Bristol, Rhode Island, designed the 22-foot keel catboat* Iris *in 1889. She scaled 24½' LOA, 22' LWL and 4½' draft with 5¾' headroom in the cabin. Her keel contained 4,822 pounds of lead ballast along with a 28-gallon water tank. Her galley was located forward and lighted by a round port in the cabin roof. Although hardly distinguishable, except for the cat rig, from a keel sloop of her day, her hull form forward bears some resemblance to the Point or Newport boat. (Herreshoff Collection, Hart Nautical Museum, Massachusetts Institute of Technology)*

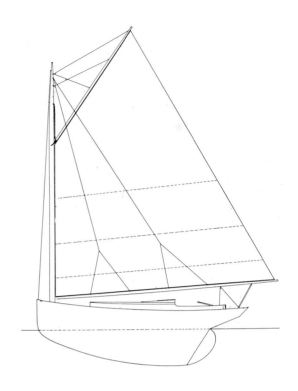

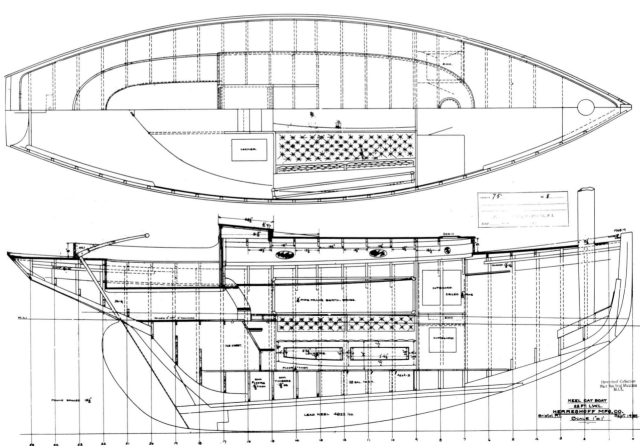

144

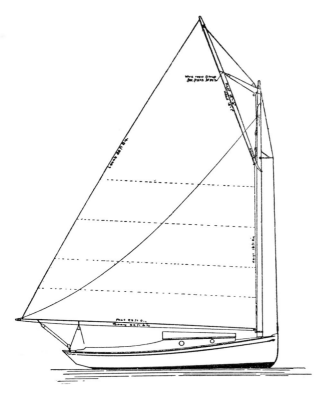

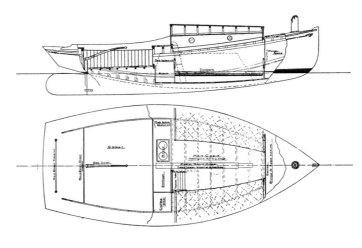

Cape Cod cat designed by Charles D. Mower. She
is 20 feet overall, 9 feet 3 inches beam, and 1 foot
7 inches draft with the board up. (Atkin, Second
Book of Boats)

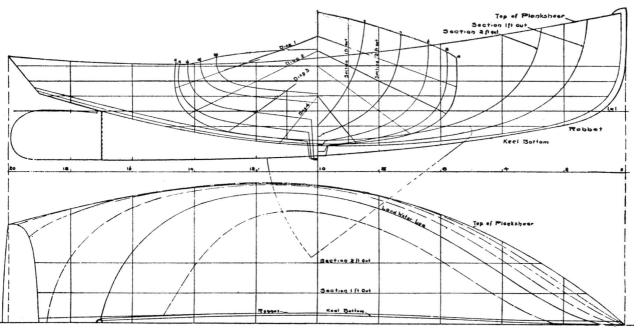

Onaway. *This gentle scene, complete with a pair of sloops and a two masted schooner, centers on Onaway, a large tumblehome stem (or canoe bow) cat of the 1880's. (Roger C. Taylor)*

Twister. *Winfield M. Thompson, a prolific writer on catboats in the early 1900's, tells the story of* Twister *in "A Catboat Sailor's Yarn," which ran in the April and May, 1906, issues of* The Rudder. *She was a 28-foot Daniel Crosby & Son's cat of the counter-stern model. She is towing* Wee Pup, *a pram of Thompson's design that became very popular in its day. (Nathaniel L. Stebbins / Society for the Preservation of New England Antiquities)*

Ward Parke's 30-foot Anderson cat Beatrice and Everett A. Poole's Anna W, both rigged for sword-fishing, lie cheek and jowl at Menemsha around 1920. Anna W's sail has slides on the luff fitting into a track on the mast. This allowed steps to be attached to the forward side of the mast so the masthead could be used as a lookout while sword-fishing. (Ward Parke)

Clara reefed. Captain Nat Herreshoff's cat yawl Clara was equipped with bat-wing sails. Long battens running from luff to leach facilitated reefing. (Nathaniel L. Stebbins / Society for the Preservation of New England Antiquities)

Mehitabel. *Roy Blaney of Boothbay Harbor, Maine, built the open cat Mehitabel in 1927 from plans said to have been published in* The Rudder *that same year. (Roy Blaney)*

Nantucket. "Pure nostalgia" is the right title for this charming, intimate scene at Old South Wharf, Nantucket, in 1891, where a large party catboat is coming in for a landing. We instinctively pull with the young lad in the velvet suit and cap as he struggles barefoot with the handsome pulling boat in the foreground. (Charles F. Sayle)

Tom. *This 30-foot cat, now owned by Arthur C. Cotta of Winthrop, Massachusetts, illustrates the sturdy work-horse characteristics that Charles Anderson (1870-1953) built into his boats at Wareham, Massachusetts, before the 1938 hurricane wiped him out. Tom probably dates from the early 1930's. The cabin house skylight is found on most big Anderson cats. (Fenwick C. Williams)*

Daysailing. A half dozen summer visitors are enjoying an outing somewhere in New England with a professional skipper, sometime in the 1890's. (The John Kochiss Collection, Mystic Seaport)

Nestor. *Steamboat Wharf, Nantucket, around 1915, with floe ice in the harbor, provides an interesting setting for* Nestor *and a companion cat.* Nestor *is rigged for scalloping, and one end of her culling board projects over her deck just abaft the cabin house. Her companion cat has a squared off cabin house forward, a feature often found in cats built before 1900. She has no bridle on her gaff. (Charles F. Sayle)*

Racing cats (left to right): Spray *and* Shearwater, *both handsome, half-decked, counter-stern cats of very sweet sheer. This early photo by the great marine photographer of his day, Nathaniel L. Stebbins, was taken in the early 1880's, possibly at a regatta of the Beverly Yacht Club, a peripatetic boating group for craft under 25-foot L.W.L. Many of the Beverly Yacht Club cats were built by Nathanael Herreshoff and, at a guess, these two lovely cats could have derived from his skillful hand.* Shearwater's *mast bends gently to the pressure of the wind. (Nathaniel L. Stebbins / Society for the Preservation of New England Antiquities)*

THE CATBOAT ASSOCIATION

Boat Name	Type	LOA	Date	Owner	Designer	Builder
Alice M.	FG	18'2	1970	M. C. Morse		Marshall
Alicia	FG	22'2	1972	C. C. Smith		Marshall
Alleluia	FG	18'2	1971	E. T. Atkinson		Marshall
Alley Cat		21'	1936	J. R. Smith		Norton
Almost	FG	18'2	1970	R.M. Clarke		Marshall
Alsea	decked-cuddy	16'	1922	M.D. Birch		Bigelow
America	FG	18'2	1972	S.J. Nowak	H. C. Herreshoff	Nowak & Williams
Americat 22	FG	22'	1971	G. Benedict	Sweisguth	Benedict-Loughlin
Anacot II	FG	22'2	1973	S. A. Flynn		Marshall
Annie		20'	1925	H. P. Wilmerding		M. S. Roberts
Apple Jack		21'9	1947	J. J. Wheeler		Hubert Johnson
Applejack	FG	18'2	1964	J. W. Wier		Marshall
Awashonks	FG	18'2	1971	L. A. Harrington		Marshall
Baccalieu	decked	16'	1927	J. A. Tuck		M. S. Roberts
Baclaju		18'	1926	J. W. Fellows		Shivrick
Bad Gnu	hard chine	18'9	1969	D. C. Pailler	Wittholz	Pailler
Baggywrinkle		23'	1908	J. L. Butera		Phinney
Barnacle		23'	1918	J. F. Macbeth		D. Crosby & Sons
Bat		29'	1924	B. T. Connolly	Chas. Mower	H. Johnson
Bay Berry	FG	18'2	1973	W. Corney		Marshall
Bay Rum	FG	18'2	1971	M. W. Keeler		Marshall
Bearcat	FG	18'2	1969	J. W. McCalley		Marshall
Beerbubble	FG	18'2	1966	E. Thompson		Marshall
Betsy II		22'	1925	W. A. Brink	Arthur Doane	N. E. Shpbldg. Co.
Betsy Ross	FG	18'2	1972	J.C. Pressey	H. C. Herreshoff	Nowak & Williams
Beubelle	FG	18'2	1972	R. G. Rode	H. C. Herreshoff	Nowak & Williams
Bimbo		18'	1954	H. Sawyer	Alden	Clark Mills
Blue Jean II	FG	18'2	1971	D. J. Sawtelle		Marshall
Blue Willow	FG	17'	1968	F. X. Flaherty	Wittholz	Hermann
Boatswain	FG	22'2	1970	P. Swain		Marshall
Bobcat	hard chine	21'9	1962	R. W. Rieger	Wittholz	Speiser
Breezing Up	FG	22'2	1972	H. E. Marx		Marshall
Broadbill	FG	18'2	1970	W. G. Cogger		Marshall
Button		20'	1969	H. E. Howes	F. Williams	Bud Brown
Buxom Lass of Salem		18'1	1949	J. W. Liener	Liener	Liener
Calico	cat yawl	23'8	c1900	G. W. Monjeau		unknown
Calico Cat	FG	18'2	1966	Needham		Marshall
Callipygia	FG	22'2	1966	T. Stetson	Marshall	Vaitses
Calynda	cat yawl	28'	1932	A. A. Northrop	Alden	Bigelow
Canard	FG	18'2	1969	J. T. Bain		Marshall
Cape Dame		23'	c1910	W. E. Schoneberger		Daniel Crosby
Carol Jean	FG	18'2	1964	W. P. Rowland		Marshall
Carol Sue	FG	17'	1971	P. J. Adams	Wittholz	Hermann

Boat Name	Type	LOA	Date	Owner	Designer	Builder
Carrie S.		15'10	1903	M. Kilpatrick		unknown
Catbird	FG	17'	1970	E. T. Harnan	Wittholz	Hermann
Catbird	FG	18'2	1966	L. Hershfield		Marshall
Catherine	FG	18'2	1963	C. J. Schreiber		Marshall
Catnap		24'	1957	Sea Explorer	Warner	Baums Btyd.
Cattail	FG	17'	1970	J. B. McMann	Wittholz	Hermann
Checkmate	FG	18'2	1970	D. B. Crosby		Marshall
Cheshire	FG	22'2	1969	E. F. Sherman		Marshall
Cimba		25'	1965	A. Van Riper	Williams	Baum
Clara F.	FG	17'	1968	W. H. Barker	Wittholz	Hermann
Comfy	FG	18'2	1967	F. B. Snow		Marshall
Compass Rose		22'4	1917	H. E. Replogle		D. Crosby & Sons
Compromise		23'11	1951	M. E. Bradford	Spkmn & Stephens	Freept. Pt. Shp.
Condorito	FG	18'2	1972	R. G. Walker		Marshall
Conjurer		27'	1909	R. Grosvenor		Crosby
Copycat	decked	14'	1972	B. L. Little		Catboats Unltd.
Corina	FG	17'		R. Kohn	Wittholz	Hermann
Corlaer	hard chine	17'1	1965	J. G. Sullivan	Wittholz	Marston-Hackett
Crispy	FG	18'2	1972	N. C. Lindeman	Herreshoff	Nowak & Williams
Crystal		18'1	1951	P. G. Chapman	Alden	Marston
Cumbrae		21'	1947	L. S. Brown	Williams	H. Johnson
Curlew		21'	1948	R. B. Andersen	Deeds	Knutsen
Cygnus		20'6	c1912	D. S. Schell		Wilton Crosby
D Wee Cat	hard chine	17'2	1970	C. W. Schmitt	Wittholz	Marston
Dauntless		20'	1920	T. R. Morey		Phinney
Defiant	FG	22'2	1971	H. D. Kerman		Marshall
Dionis	FG	22'2	1966	T. A. McGraw		Marshall
Dolphin		21'5	1917	A. K. Lane		Wilton Crosby
Dolphin		28'	1893	R. W. Wilkerson		Huxford
Do-Me		24'		R. L. Reddington		H & A Crosby
Dorothy	FG	18'2	1971	G. L. Turnpaugh		Marshall
Dovekie	FG	18'2	1971	R. Snyder		Marshall
Dowitcher	FG	18'2	1965	S. W. Satterlee		Marshall
Duckling	FG	17'	1969	R. H. Reibel	Wittholz	Hermann
Dulcinea	FG	22'2	1969	J. Marinovich		Marshall
Dulcinea	FG	22'2	1972	J. Wolter		Marshall
Dutch Treat	FG	18'2	1972	P. B. Zwiers	H. Herreshoff	Nowak & Williams
Easy	FG	18'2	1969	S. W. Randolph		Marshall
Edwina B.		22'	1931	G. J. L. Griswold		M. S. Roberts
Elizabeth	FG	22'2	1966	R. Viall	Marshall	Moses Zubee
Ella Marie	decked	16'	c1930	E. S. Pratt	Thompson	Thompson & Brown
El-Mar-Oscuro	FG	18'2	1973	B. C. Doust		Marshall
Emma B.		25'	1966	R. C. Reese	Wittholz	Finkeldey
Eventide		29'10	1933	F. O. Walther		Shivrick
Falcon		17'3	1931	G. S. Egeland		Will Smith
Fancy Smile	FG	18'2	1963	D. S. Fishman		Marshall
Fat Cat	FG	18'2	1971	R. W. Noll		Marshall
Felicia	FG	18'2	1969	E. C. Chapin		Marshall
Felicity		25'2	1969	W. L. Burling	Wittholz	Blaney

Boat Name	Type	LOA	Date	Owner	Designer	Builder
Feline	hard chine	17'1	1961	P. J. Stueck	Wittholz	Marston
Felinity	FG	18'2	1968	J. I. Babbitt		Marshall
Felix	FG	22'2	1968	B. B. Brewster		Marshall
Felix	FG	17'	1972	R. B. Miles	Wittholz	Hermann
Ferlie		18'10	1891	E. D. Hamilton	Bliven	
Fiddler	FG	18'2	1964	D. Helfrich		Marshall
Fiddler		19'	1950	D. A. Lewis	Williams	Kittery Pt. Btyd.
Figaro		18'3	1972	B. M. Levine		Simonsen
Fiona		16'	1957	P. E. Guernsey		Auregson
Fireman's Bride		22'	1900?	C. Hugg		Dan Crosby
Flying Colors	FG	18'2	1972	P. A. Burckmyer	Herreshoff	Nowak & Wms.
Frances		20'8	1968	T. Hornor		Wilton Crosby
Free Spirit		20'	1955	R. E. Alling		Marston
Friend	FG	22'2	1967	J. Donnelly		Marshall
Frolic		26'	1925	A. W. Rockwood		H. Manley Crosby
Galatea		24'6	1935	L. J. Benoit	F. S. Dunbar	Crosby Yt. Bldg.
Gallia IV	FG	18'2	1966	G. N. Litwin		Marshall
Gannet		22'	1920	K. J. Aspenberg		Crosby
Gannet	FG	18'2	1972	D. C. Twichell		Marshall
Gata Gorda	FG	18'2	1970	L. R. Clapp	Marshall	L. R. Clapp
Gay Head		22'	1927	F. C. Wood		Richard Norton
Geraldine		20'	1940	J. M. Montgomery		Geo. F. Carter
Ginger		18'	1955	T. C. Schuyler	Williams	Lund Bt. Wks.
Golden Years	hard chine	17'1	1961	A. A. Morais	Wittholz	(Japan)
Good Return	FG	22'2	1971	P. H. McCormick		Marshall
Gracie	FG	18'2	1972	C. Storrow		Marshall
Grayling	FG	22'2	1965	J. H. Walton		Marshall
Grey Gull	FG	18'2	1965	J. P. Gilligan		Marshall
Grimalkin	FG	22'2	1965	R. W. Jones		Marshall
Grimalkin	FG	18'2	1970	N. E. Wood		Marshall
Gull Cry	hard chine	14'10	1964	R. D. Lewis	Wittholz	Marston
Half n' Half	FG	18'2	1968	H. H. Fehr		Marshall
Hannah Screecham		18'	1942	Malatesta		
Happy Herman	FG	17'	1968	M. MacKinnon	Wittholz	Hermann
Happy Jack		21'	1938	J. Llewellyn		Phinney
Hard Tack		22'	1939	T. G. Hyland	Robertson	
Harriet W.		21'11½	1971	J. F. Elsaesser		Wind Ships
H. B. Gul Rose		17'	1930	W. P. Abbe		M. S. Roberts
Heather	decked	14'	1937	J. W. McPherson		Crosby Yt. Bldg.
Hebe	FG	18'2	1967	B. Smith		Marshall
Helter II		15'	c1920	R. F. Brownlie		
Honey	FG	18'2	1969	J. Wight		Marshall
Honey Jo		18'		R. H. Oeschger		Shivrick
Horatio		22'	1910	E. Dorbandt		Wilton Crosby
Ilona	FG	18'2	1969	J. B. Davis		Marshall
Imagine!	FG	18'2	1972	R. F. Fleischhauer	Herreshoff	Nowak & Wms.
Imp	decked	14'4	1911	D. E. Woehler	E. B. Schock	Church
Jerseybelle	decked	19'	1931	D. P. Charnews		Johnson (N.J.)
Joda	FG	18'2	1971	R. G. Sadler		Marshall
Jubilation	FG	22'2		P. E. T. Drumm		Marshall

156

Boat Name	Type	LOA	Date	Owner	Designer	Builder
Judy		25'6	1927	H. H. Eddy		Daniel Crosby
Kayo		16'6	1968	B. A. Smith		Clark Mills
Kelpie	FG	18'2	1969	J. W. Borden		Marshall
Ketch Katt	cat ketch	26'	1908	H. D. Fairchild		prob. Crosby
Kiddie Kat		30'	1927	J. C. Freeburg		Anderson
Kit Kat	FG	22'2	1966	W. Garfield	Marshall	Grinnell
Kitten	FG	17'	1969	N. Card	Wittholz	Hermann
Kitten		20'	1903	R. L. Cyr		Herb. Crosby
Kittiwake	hard chine	15'6	1960	R. A. Hill	Wittholz	Wstbrk. Bt. & Eng.
Kittiwake	FG	22'2	1972	R. N. Sears		Marshall
Kittiwake	FG	18'2	1969	A. H. Sutliffe		Marshall
Kitty		18'9	1960	A. A. Gangell	Wittholz	Jela-Yugoslavia
Kitty Kelly		18'	1972	F. S. Cassidy	Williams	Briggs-Cassidy
Knot		20'	1905	G. H. Abbot		Crosby
Lady Lou V		22'	1936	J. D. Beinert	Sweisguth	Haff
La Mouette	FG	18'2	1971	D. S. Brown		Marshall
Lilla III	FG	18'2	1972	C. L. Seitz	Herreshoff	Nowak & Wms.
Lilly Y.	decked	14'3	c1935	J. V. Linebaugh		unknown
Little Albie	FG	18'2	1970	H. R. Stevenson		Marshall
Little Bear	FG	17'	1968	T. S. Farmer	Wittholz	Hermann
Little Lady		17'	1960	P. J. McHugh	Wittholz	Reginald Bourne
Little Liza	FG	18'2	1971	E. A. Rogers		Marshall
Little Nell	FG	18'2	1964	R. C. Philbrick		Marshall
Lively Lady	FG	18'2	1966	J. P. Bertelsen		Marshall
Lobelia		20'6	1965	J. W. Anderson	Williams	Little
Long Swing	FG	18'2	1972	F. Ricciardone		Marshall
Lotus		28'	1924	D. R. McShane		Crosby
Love	FG	18'2	1968	W. L. Kennedy		Marshall
Lovely Ambition	FG	18'2	1968	M. Anschutz		Marshall
Madakat	FG	22'2	1973	C. Pollak		Marshall
Mad Catter	FG	17'	1968	M. J. Wisniewski		Hermann
Magnolia	FG	22'2	1966	W. S. Drew		Marshall
Mahi Mahi		20'4	1965	S. Miki	Yokoyama	Okazaki Bt. Yd.
Manx		22'	1930	R. F. Dunlop	Sweisguth	
Manx	FG	18'2	1972	F. L. Kelsch	H. Herreshoff	Nowak & Wms.
Margaret Mary		25'	1900	J. B. Wehrlen		Crosby
Mari Lyn	FG	18'2	1967	J. S. Entwisle		Marshall
Marionette	decked	14'5	1888	B. Stuart		Edgar Jenny
Mascot		25'8	1930	W. F. Gallagher		Johnson
Maureen		41'	1926	R. E. Alling		Crosby
Mehitabel	FG	22'2	1970	R. Hayden		Marshall
Melody	FG	22'2	1968	T. Loizeaux		Marshall
Memory	cat yawl	28'	1935	J. Pickering	Williams	Vnyd. Hvn. Shpbd.
Meow	ferro cement	32'	1970	T. H. Holmes	Holmes	Seacrete
Merrie Mag	FG	22'2	1968	R. P. Owsley		Marshall
Merry Thought		27'	1907	F. M. Middleton		H. Manley Crosby
Merry Tune	FG	18'2	1967	C. B. Barclay		Marshall
Mickle		15'	1962	R. P. Dunlop	Goeller	H. C. Wethey
Mincie		16'		P. C. Morris		
Miss America	FG	18'2	1972	J. E. Martenhoff	Herreshoff	Nowak & Wms.

Boat Name	Type	LOA	Date	Owner	Designer	Builder
Mi-Yot		18'2	1972	H. A. Cooper		Wstbrk. Bt. & Eng.
Mollie B.	cat yawl	27'6	1927	P. G. Birdsall	Hanley	Baker Yt. Basin
Mooncusser	FG	18'2	1965	F. P. Wales		Marshall
Mother Courage	FG	18'2	1971	P. D. Fleischman		Marshall
Mug		22'		W. L. Jones		
Myan	FG	18'2	1970	D. G. Heenehan		Marshall
Naiad		24'		L. H. Munkelwitz		D. & H. Crosby
Nana	FG	17'	1967	N. G. Alford	Wittholz	Hermann
Nauta	FG	18'2	1965	R. H. Hutchinson		Marshall
Necromancer		19'6	1973	W. C. Gref	Skinner	Gref
Nifty	FG	18'2	1969	G. Angier		Marshall
Nixie	FG	18'2	1968	A. W. Frank		Marshall
no name	FG	18'2		W. T. Brawner		Marshall
no name	FG	22'2	1969	P. L. Brown		Marshall
no name	decked	14'3	1971	M. S. Hammatt		Areys Pd. Btyd.
no name	FG	22'2	1971	C. W. Huff		Marshall
no name	FG	22'2	1970	B. H. Keenan		Marshall
no name		17'1	1963	J. H. Lowe	Wittholz	Wstbrk. Bt. & Eng.
no name	FG	18'2		K. E. Nicholson		Marshall
no name	FG	22'2	1972	G. S. Smith		Marshall
no name	FG	18'2	1969	T. A. Stowe		Marshall
no name	FG	18'2	1971	G. T. Thomson		Marshall
no name	FG	22'2	1972	A. Ulrich		Marshall
no name		20'	1907	R. G. Whitelaw		Dan'l Crosby
Nugget	hard chine	15'	1966	E. M. Pieters	Wittholz	Trevor-Lewis
Off Islander	decked	17'		C. A. Johnson		Butler
Old Bill		22'	1937	L. Goyette	Mower	Cotter
Olé	FG	18'2	1966	E. D. Madigan		Marshall
Oslaug		20'	1920	L. M. Crowell		Wilton Crosby
Pamir IV	FG	22'	1971	R. Meier	Gilgenast	Michelsen (Germ.)
Patchy Fog		18'	1955	C. H. Buckley	Alden	Story
Peg's Cat	hard chine	19'1	1961	P. E. Bendicksen	Wittholz	Jela-Yugoslavia
Pelican		24'	1930	E. W. Lombard		Casey Bt. Bldg.
Pelican	FG	17'	1968	R. B. McCagg	Wittholz	Hermann
Pelican		23'7	1908	J. W. Pence		Chas. H. Crosby
Penelope	FG	18'2	1970	A. Kovacs		Marshall
Pinafore		20'4	1957	R. C. Smith		Geo. Frank Carter
Peregrin Q.	FG	17'	1972	D. E. Lowe	Benford	Lowe
Pinkletink		21'11	1932	J. M. Leavens		H. F. Crosby & Son
Platypuss	FG	22'2	1972	M. L. Cramer		Marshall
Plautus		26'	1909	R. Cousins		Crosby
Playpen	FG	18'2		M. H. Daniell		Marshall
Plum Duff		15'	1958	R. Haworth		Haworth
Polly Anne	FG	18'2	1970	J. Messick		Marshall
Polly C.		18'	1921	R. P. Allingham		
Polpis		20'	1932	R. M. Packer		Erford Burt
Priscilla	FG	18'2	1972	J. S. Van Orden		Marshall
Prudence		25'2	1959	S. A. Mitchell	Wittholz	Blaney
Puffin	FG	18'2	1970	A. Cuenin		Marshall
Pufnstuf	FG	17'	1971	E. Soesbe	Wittholz	Hermann

158

Boat Name	Type	LOA	Date	Owner	Designer	Builder
Pumpkin	decked	14'3	1910	P. T. Vermilya		Anderson
Purr Puss	decked	14'	1895	J. H. Kreisher		Crosby
Pussy Cat		24'	1924	A. Troge		M. S. Roberts
Pywacket		25'6	1972	R. S. Jerrell	Wittholz	Jerrell
Quahog	FG	18'2	1963	S. L. Wright		Marshall
Que Pasa		18'	1959	O. P. Morton	Williams	
Red Squirrel	FG	22'2	1973	N. Lund		Marshall
Rip Van Winkle	FG	18'2	1973	J. G. Harris		Marshall
Ruth Pauline		16'6	1920	J. P. Van Lieu	Goeller	
Saint Brendan	FG	18'2	1967	J. F. Saburn		Marshall
Salavin		20'4	1965	K. Kitagawa	Yokoyama	Okazaki Bt. Yd.
Sally		21'2	1929	E. Homsey		H. Manley Crosby
Sandpiper		18'6	1936	L. H. Christie		Roberts
Scat	FG	22'2	1969	H. S. Geneen		Marshall
Scoter	FG	22'	1971	G. W. Martinson	Sweisguth	Benedict-Loughlin
Scoter		20'6	1955	S. Reynolds	Williams	Marston
Sea Cat		30'	1936	A. C. Cotta		Anderson
Sea Fire II		22'	1957	H. Heap	Crocker	MacIntosh
Sea Horse		22'9	1910	H. S. Goodwin		Ch. Crosby
Sea Hound		25'9	1911	R. C. Ascher		Ch. Crosby
Sea Lady		25'11	1913	H. Jennings		Wilton Crosby
Sea Mew	FG	18'2	1972	J. C. Cashman	H. Herreshoff	Nowak & Wms.
Sea Oats		21'	c1930	F. E. Elliott		Chas. Crosby
Sea Pup		21'	1937	L. B. Bedell		M. S. Roberts
Seaweed	FG	22'2	1970	C. F. Bullock		Marshall
Sea Wyf	FG	18'2	1965	W. T. Lindquist		Marshall
Secret		22'6	1927	L. H. Brown	Sweisguth	Haft
Selina II		41'6	1927	B. Hunt		H. W. Sweet Shpyd.
Serendipity	hard chine	17'	1960	E. W. Jones	Wittholz	Marston
Serendipity	FG	18'2	1966	H. A. Schneider		Marshall
Simplicity	FG	18'2	1970	R. L. Michelson		Marshall
Sinbad		21'	1922	J. Shultz		Crosby
Sitzmark		19'6	1964	W. F. Hilton	W. J. Skinner	Hilton
Smuggler	FG	18'2	1972	P. Fagnano		Marshall
Snuffy	FG	18'2	1964	J. H. Riley		Marshall
Solon		20'4	1966	H. Ishikawa	Yokoyama	Okazaki Bt. Yd.
Sour Puss	FG	22'2	1969	C. B. Horne		Marshall
Southwind		35'	1902	R. S. Stowe		Wilton Crosby
South Wind II	FG	18'2	1966	A. M. Blackman		Marshall
Spanky	FG	18'2	1969	C. Beran		Marshall
Spindrift	hard chine	17'	1965	R. R. Bachman	Wittholz	Marston
Spoon Drift	FG	18'2	1964	P. Richmond		Marshall
Spray	FG	18'2	1972	T. Dill	H. Herreshoff	Nowak & Wms.
Spray		22'		M. Osmond		Crosby
Sprite	FG	17'	1969	J. F. Fargason	Wittholz	Hermann
Stormalong	FG	18'2	1970	J. P. Brodsky		Marshall
Storm King		20'	1903	D. S. Wadsworth		Dan Crosby
Stormy Petrel		24'	1930	W. Pfohl	F. C. Williams	Pfohl
Strawberry Fields Forever	FG	17'	1967	D. McCabe	Wittholz	Hermann

Boat Name	Type	LOA	Date	Owner	Designer	Builder
Sunshine III		27'	pre 1916	R. B. Marshall		Dan Crosby
Susan		22'6	1929	W. J. Urban		Deering
Suzy B.		19'	1966	S. N. Baker	Wittholz	A. G. Merrill
Swan II	FG	18'2	1969	P. L. Wilds		Marshall
Sylph	FG	17'	1971	O. E. Schlauch	Wittholz	Hermann
Tabitha	FG	22'2	1965	L. E. Williams		Marshall
Tambourine		21'	1963	W. Blake	Williams	MacIntosh
Tam o' Shanter		25'9	1963	D. H. Putnam	McGinnis	Grinnel
Tang		24'	1910	G. S. Frierson		Crosby
Teal		22'	1927	S. L. Goldsmith		Dexter Bros.
Tempter	FG	18'2	1971	M. B. Patterson		Marshall
The Cat	FG	18'2	1971	J. Alves		Marshall
The Gull	FG	22'2	1968	P. L. Troast		Marshall
The Old Sculpin		22'	1946	K. G. Roos		M. S. Roberts
The Ugly Duckling		17'	c1907	J. L. O'Brien		
Thordis	cat yawl	33'4	1897	J. J. Maselli	Hanley	
Tigger	FG	22'2	1971	J. Parker & C. McKim		Marshall
Tinker	FG	22'2	1967	W. R. Reid		Marshall
Tinkerbelle		18'3	1912	E. J. Keenan		
Tom Cat	FG	18'2	1968	J. A. D'Agostino		Marshall
Tom Cat	FG	18'2	1966	J. R. Judson		Marshall
Topcat	FG	18'2	1972	C. W. Bevier	H. Herreshoff	Nowak & Wms.
Top Cat	FG	22'2	1973	R. T. McCabe		Marshall
Tortuga		23'	c1890	R. S. Bruno		Crosby
Tradition	FG	18'2	1963	N. H. Halliday		Marshall
Tradition		24'	1910	E. Rattray		Crosby
Tranquility		19'	1968	J. L. McCaffrey	Wittholz	Wm. Simonsen
Tranquil Lady		17'3	1915	B. D. Grossman		M. S. Roberts
Trim Again		24'	1959	L. C. Hill	McGinnis	Long, Ryder
Tyche	FG	17'	1968	R. Goodhart	Wittholz	Hermann
Ups n' Downs	FG	18'2	1967	C. W. Downs		Marshall
Valiant		22'	c1920	C. A. Peek		Chas. Crosby
Valma	FG	18'2	1968	R. A. Allain		Marshall
Vanity		20'8	1929	O. C. Pease		M. S. Roberts
Venture II	FG	22'2	1967	T. S. Curtis		Marshall
Victoria	FG	17'	1971	J. R. Mills	Wittholz	Cape Cod Ship Bld.
Victoria		18'	1963	N. Pott	Carter	Cheoy Lee Shpyd.
Victory		20'	1910	C. A. Crosby & E. M. Crosby		Wilton Crosby
Wasis III		21'	1938	R. A. Moll		Mosher
Watermelon		23'	1928	J. Arecco		
Wee Mac	hard chine	17'	1961	J. S. Macgregor	Wittholz	Marston
Whimsy	FG	18'2	1968	W. Van Winkle		Marshall
Wild Swan	FG	22'2	1966	J. B. Mims		Marshall
Will o' th' Wind	FG	18'2	1965	J. Waterbury		Marshall
Window Blind		15'	1968	W. F. O'Donnell	Wittholz	Geo. Warren
Wink IV	FG	22'2	1973	R. W. Mechem		Marshall
Winsome Wiggy		24'	1912	A. E. Symonds		M. S. Roberts
Wynnsong	hard chine	20'	1968	A. M. Thewlis		Thewlis
Yankee		15'8	c1930	H. W. Austin		Anderson
Zim III	FG	22'2	1970	W. B. Mize		Marshall